PRISONS THE WORLD OVER

PRISONS THE WORLD OVER

Rita J. Simon and Christiaan A. de Waal

LEXINGTON BOOKS

A division of
ROWMAN & LITTLEFIELD PUBLISHERS, INC.
Lanham • Boulder • New York • Toronto • Oxford

Published by Lexington Books
A division of Rowman & Littlefield Publishers, Inc.
A wholly owned subsidary of The Rowman & Littlefield Publishing Group, Inc.
4501 Forbes Boulevard, Suite 200, Lanham, Maryland 20706
http://www.lexingtonbooks.com

Estover Road, Plymouth PL6 7PY, United Kingdom

British Library Cataloguing in Publication Information Available

Library of Congress Cataloging-in-Publication Data

Simon, Rita J. (Rita James), 1931–
    Prisons the world over / Rita J. Simon and Christiaan A. de Waal.
        p. cm.
    Includes bibliographical references and index.
    ISBN 978-0-7391-4024-6 (cloth : alk. paper) — ISBN 978-0-7391-4026-0 (electronic)
    1. Prisons. 2. Prisoners. I. Waal, Christiaan A. de, 1981– II. Title.
HV8665.S49 2009
365—dc22   2009023162

⊗ ™ The paper used in this publication meets the minimum requirements of American
National Standard for Information Sciences—Permanence of Paper for Printed Library
Materials, ANSI/NISO Z39.48-1992.

Printed in the United States of America

Contents

Part Five: Middle East

Part Six: Africa

Part Seven: Asia

Part Eight: Oceania

Introduction

P*RISONS THE WORLD OVER* is the 13th book in the series on comparative analysis of social issues and problems in different societies spread throughout the world. Earlier volumes have analyzed abortion laws and practices, euthanasia, death penalty, pornography, marriage and divorce, education, juvenile justice systems, drug trafficking, the roles and statuses of women, the defense of insanity, voting and elections, and the rights and responsibilities of citizenship. The countries included in this volume are: the United States, Canada, Argentina, Brazil, France, Germany, Great Britain, Italy, Sweden, Hungary, Poland, Russia, Israel, Egypt, Iran, Nigeria, South Africa, India, China, Japan, and Australia.

To the extent that data are available, in *Prisons the World Over*, we report the number of prisoners, the rate per population, and the percent of female prisoners across the 21 countries included in the study along with the number of penal institutions, their occupancy level and the presence and number of privately run prisons. Other issues reported are the offenses for which the inmates are interred, the average length of incarceration, the availability of parole, conditions in the prisons, the availability of educational and work programs, provisions for children of female prisoners, the availability and quality of medical care, the characteristics of the prison staff, and the visitation rights of prisoners.

As of 2007, more than 9.25 million people were imprisoned worldwide. Almost half of the persons imprisoned are in the United States, China, and Russia. Since the beginning of the 1990s, the prison population has increased significantly. Before providing a country-by-country analysis, we offer a brief account of the history of prisons, a discussion of international standards, and an analysis of private prisons.

Prisons: A Brief History

It was not until the twelfth century that prisons were widely used for punishment or as a place of rehabilitation. Before then, prisons were primarily a place that held and controlled individuals while they awaited trial or punishment. It was in the sixteenth century that the goals for a prison included rehabilitation along with extended incarceration within the confines of the prisons. There was no separation by age, sex, or convicted status.[1]

Attempts at improving conditions in European prisons began with the work of John Howard in the late eighteenth century. Howard found that prisoners were often starved, had no bedding and lived in very crowded, filthy conditions. After he testified before the House of Commons, the Jail Act of 1774 was passed. It suggested ways for improving sanitation and did away with the fees paid by inmates to jailers for their room and board.

In 1789, the first prison was built in the United States, the Walnut Street jail in Philadelphia. During the 1880s, two types of prisons emerged in America and then spread to Europe. In 1817, the Auburn system was instituted. In this system, the prisoners worked together all day in silence, but were housed separately at night. This system was criticized for being just short of slavery, as prisoners were often put to work for private industries that took advantage of inexpensive prison labor. In 1829, the Pennsylvania system was instituted, which was simply solitary confinement, 24 hours a day. Most of the states opted for the Auburn system because of the economic opportunity it provided.

By the 1920s, in part out of humanitarian concerns and in part because prison labor was too competitive, the Auburn system was severely restricted. In the late 1930s, several laws were passed to restrict prison labor in order to free up the labor market.

When the idea of labor as a form of rehabilitation ended, the idea of personal rehabilitation began. Social scientists sought to provide methods by which prisoners could be classified according to their likelihood of rehabilitation, so that their specific needs could be met. By the 1960s, the emphasis on rehabilitation continued and was extended to include community-based corrections, diversion programs, work-release programs, and probation centers.

The idea of reforming the individual had its origin during the early eighteenth century with Cesare Beccaria of Italy, who argued against the harsh punishment being imposed on inmates. As writers began to consider the ideology behind punishment, and began to consider mitigating circumstances surrounding a crime, as well as the legal and moral responsibility of criminals, the various levels of punishment suited to individual needs began to evolve. The increasing emphasis on rehabilitation as opposed to punishment is demonstrated by the emergence of the concepts of parole, probation, indeterminate sentences, and the institution of juvenile courts and reformatories. Emphasis began to be placed on rehabilitation for "the good of society and the individual," rather than on punishment for its own sake. Although other methods of punishment have developed, incarceration is still heavily practiced. The prison as we know it today has emerged through changes in purpose and design. Although the idea of imprisonment for punishment and rehabilitation is global, every country has a different method for instituting it.

International Standards

In 1934 the League of Nations adopted a series of rules developed by the International Penal and Penitentiary Commission, now known as the United Nations Standard Minimum Rules for the Treatment of Prisoners (SMRTP). It was not until 1957, however, that the rules were formally approved by the UN Economic and Social Council. This set of rules or standards regarding prison conditions and the treatment of prisoners is not legally binding, because of varying ways countries around the world manage their prison systems. Because not all the rules could be applied to all penal systems around the world, they outlined what is generally accepted as being good principle and practice in prisoner treatment and prison management. Although this set of standards is not a formal code, it is expected that every nation will attempt to achieve the minimum conditions accepted by the United Nations. The SMRTP have been updated to better address current conditions. The UN General Assembly also adopted the Basic Principles of the Treatment of Prisoners. A similar set of rules was developed by the Council of Europe in 1973, called the European Prison Rules (ERP). These rules are much like those in SMRTP, but they were developed to coordinate better with the European penal system.

The SMRTP generally provide the following: prisoners should be separated by sex, type of crime, age, conviction status; cells for individuals should not be used to accommodate more than two persons overnight; prisoners should be provided with adequate water and toiletries and be required to keep themselves clean; prisoners not allowed to wear their own clothing should be provided with suitable clothing and provisions for laundry; every prisoner should be provided with a separate bed and sufficient bedding; wholesome, well-prepared food is to be provided to prisoners at regular hours; drinking water should be provided to prisoners whenever needed; if not assigned outdoors to work, every prisoner shall have at least one hour of exercise outdoors; a medical officer with some knowledge of psychiatry and a qualified dental officer is to be available to every institution; prenatal and postnatal care and treatment are to be provided in women's institutions; every prison shall maintain a library for prisoners with recreational and instructional books; prison personnel are to be sufficiently educated, and receive ongoing courses and training; to the extent possible, prison personnel should include psychiatric, social work, and educational professionals; personnel are to be able to speak the language of the greatest number of prisoners and are to retain the services of an interpreter when necessary.

The ERP generally provides for the following: prisoners should be treated impartially without regard to race, color, religion, or sex; inspections should occur on a regular basis of all penal institutions to ensure they comply with all existing rules and regulations; standards and regulations shall be available to staff and prisoners; standards and regulations shall be available in as many languages as necessary and should be made available to staff and prisoners; individual cells should be available and shared accommodations should be supervised; all sleeping accommodations shall meet the requirements of health and hygiene; adequate bathing and shower facilities should be available; provisions should be made to allow prisoners to cut their hair and beards; prisoners not allowed to wear their own clothing shall be provided with suitable clothing; prisoners should be provided with meals that satisfy in quality and quantity the standards of modern dietetics and hygiene and take into account age, health, and to the extent possible, religious and cultural requirements; every institution shall have at least one qualified doctor and shall provide psychiatric and dental care; experiments that may result in physical or moral injury are banned; accommodations should be made for children to be born outside the institution in a hospital or, if not possible, that a qualified staff and suitable accommodations are available; prison staff should receive continuous training to comply with all standards and regulations; prisoners should be allowed to work in jobs that resemble as closely as possible the work they would do in a community; prisoners must have at least one rest day per week and must be given time for education, treatment, and immersion programs for reintegration into the community; prisoners shall be compensated for their work and may use earnings to purchase provisions in the prison or to provide for their families; a comprehensive education program should be available in every institution and should be as mandated and regimented as work; remedial education should be provided and special attention paid to the educational needs of young prisoners, those of foreign origin, or those with particular ethnic or cultural needs; every prison should have an adequately stocked library; every prisoner shall be allowed adequate exercise and recreational activities; and prisoners who are in custody but have not been convicted should be held in the least restrictive manner possible.

Both sets of rules are similar in that their main concern is with the sanitation, hygiene, health, work, education, and overall humane treatment of individuals. Most countries included in this volume satisfy some or most of the conditions described above to varying degrees. Although prison is considered a form of punishment in modern times, it ought not impose undue harm on the prisoner. These rules are simply an attempt to ensure that a minimum standard of living conditions and treatment is provided to each inmate.

Private Prisons

A private prison is an institution in which inmates are physically confined for profit. Private prison companies usually enter into contractual agreements with local, state, or federal governments that commit prisoners and then pay a per diem or monthly rate for each prisoner confined in the facility.

There are private prisons in the United States, Canada (as of 2006), the United Kingdom, Germany (one private facility as of 2005), Australia, New Zealand, Israel (one private facility as of 2005), and South Africa.

As of 2006, data indicate that Australia has the largest population of prisoners held in private prisons, and the United States has the largest number of private prisons. In Australia in 1996, 2,500 prisoners, or 15 percent of the total prison population, were in private prisons. The private facilities are located in four states: Queensland, New South Wales, Victoria, and South Australia.

The United Kingdom has the most privatized prison system in Europe; about 10 percent of the prisoners in the United Kingdom are detained in 11 private prisons. Although there are not as many private facilities as in the United States, the proportion of prisoners in private prisons is larger. In 1996, South Africa opened its first private prison. As of 2000, plans were afoot to open additional private prisons.

The United States was the first country to open private prisons, followed by Australia and the United Kingdom. The largest operator of private prisons in the United States is the Correctional Corporation of America (CCA). As of 2008, it had 65 facilities under management, including 40 it owned outright that housed 72,000 inmates.

San Quentin prison in California, which opened in 1852, was the first privately run facility in the United States. But after a number of major scandals surfaced concerning the management of the facility, California turned San Quentin over to the control of the state government.

As of 2008, there were 264 privately owned correctional facilities that house some 99,000 adult offenders. In addition to the CCA, which operates the largest number of private prisons, two other major companies are the Cornell Companies which house 19,226 inmates in 79 facilities and the GEO Groups which operates 61 facilities that contain 49,000 inmates. The states that have the greatest number of private prisons are Texas, California, Florida, and Colorado. But in total, less than 5 percent of all inmates are housed in private facilities in the United States.

The major research findings on private prisons are summarized below.

- Privately operated prisons function as well as publicly operated prisons.
- Operating costs of privately owned prisons can reduce expenditures in markets where public employee benefits are high.
- Management problems in privatized prisons are linked to poorly drafted contracts, lack of oversight and improperly classified transfer of inmates.
- Private entities can construct facilities faster and cheaper than public sector.
- Presence of private prisons has encouraged public facilities to adopt cost savings strategies in the areas of staff deployment and procurement policies.
- Majority of privately operated prisons (not jails or detention centers) are relatively new, with bed capacities of 800 or less and designed for medium and minimum custody inmates.
- Privately operated prisons function similarly to publicly owned prisons with respect to program and work participation by inmates and distribution of staff by key functional areas.
- Private facilities have lower staffing levels, lower salaries and a higher rate of assaults on staff and inmates, and they are not necessarily safer or better managed. Assaults on guards by inmates were 49 percent more frequent in private prisons than in government run prisons. The same study reported that assaults on fellow inmates were 65 percent more frequent in private prisons.

Appendix B includes three tables. Table B.1 provides a breakdown by countries of the total prison population, the rate per population, and the number of penal institutions as of October 2006. Table B.2 describes the capacity level and the occupancy level by countries. Table B.3 describes the number of female prisoners and the percent of total inmates.

We turn now to a country by country analysis.

Notes

1. Much of this discussion was adopted from a chapter written by a graduate student of Rita Simon's, Gena Barbiere, that appeared in a book Rita Simon edited, *A Comparative Perspective on Major Social Problems* (Lanham, MD: Lexington Books, 2001).

I
NORTH AMERICA

1

Canada

C ANADA BORDERS THE NORTH ATLANTIC OCEAN on the east, the North Pacific Ocean on the west, the Artic Ocean on the north, and the United States on the south. It has a population of 33,390,141 (July 2007 est.). The ethnic groups in Canada are those of British Isles origin (28 percent); mixed background (26 percent); French origin (23 percent); other European (15 percent); Amerindian (2 percent); and other, mostly Asian, African, and Arab (6 percent). The predominant religions are Roman Catholic (43 percent), Protestant (23 percent), and other (17 percent). The figures are according to the 2001 Census. Both English and French are official languages.

Canada is a constitutional monarchy that is also a parliamentary democracy. It is a federation divided into ten provinces and three territories. The authority to make laws is divided between the Parliament and the provincial legislatures. The Constitution Act of 1867 established the division of power and authority between the federal and provincial levels of government.[1]

The federal, provincial, and municipal levels of government share the responsibility for the various parts of the criminal justice system. The federal police force is concerned mainly with the enforcement of federal statutes, such as the Customs Act and Narcotic Control Act. The Canadian Parliament has been given exclusive jurisdiction with regard to passing criminal laws and developing criminal procedures. The provinces have jurisdiction over the administration of justice in each province.

Canada's legal system utilizes an inquisitorial process in some proceedings such as a coroner's inquest or a Royal Commission Inquiry, but an adversarial process is used for both civil and criminal trials. Enacted in 1892, the

Canadian Criminal Code, uniform across the country, is the basis for criminal law. But, in 1955, a totally new revised criminal code came into force.

Crimes are classified into two broad categories: those that are tried by summary conviction and those that are tried by indictment. The most serious crimes fall under the category of indictable offenses, and these crimes are punishable by at least two years imprisonment in a federal penitentiary. Summary offenses are less serious crimes. Local provinces can define these offenses and sentences can range from fines and probation, to a maximum of six months incarceration in a provincial prison. Offenses can also be hybrid offenses or dual offenses where the prosecutor has discretion to proceed by summary conviction or by indictment.

The age of criminal responsibility, as defined under the Young Offenders Act of 1985, is eighteen years old. The Parliament of Canada abolished the death penalty in 1976.

As of 2006 there were 34,244 prisoners in Canada at a rate of 107 per 100,000 population; 5 percent or 1,819 were female prisoners. Canada is second to the United States in the number of persons in prison per population. The average sentence for a person in a federal penitentiary is 46 months. There are 172 prisons in Canada and they have an occupancy level of 91.3 percent. As of 2002–2003, there were 15,000 staff members.

Correctional services expenditures totaled $2.8 billion in 2004/2005, up 2 percent in constant dollars from 2003/2004. Custodial services (prisons) accounted for the largest proportion (71 percent) of the expenditures, followed by community supervision services (14 percent), headquarters and central services (14 percent), and National Parole Board and provincial parole boards (2 percent). This figure does not include policing or court costs which bring the total expenditures up to more than $10 billion for the year.

The cost in Canadian dollars of incarceration by gender is shown below.

The major offenses for which the prisoners are interred are shown below.

Prison Conditions

The HIV infection rate among prisoners is at least 15 times higher than in the general population. There are estimates that Hepatitis C (HCV) is 50 times more prevalent in prisons than in the general population. A recent study revealed that the number of male inmates with mental health problems increased by 71 percent between 1997 and 2006 and that 12 percent of male offenders suffer from psychiatric disorders. Four out of five inmates also suffer from substance abuse problems.[2]

TABLE 1.1.

Canada: Cost in Canadian Dollars of Incarceration by Gender

Women	$150,867 million
Men	$110,223 million (maximum-security level)
	$71,640 million (medium-security level)
	$74,431 million (minimum-security level)

Source: Correctional Service of Canada, 2005

TABLE 1.2.

Canada: Prisoners by Offense Type, 2001

Offense Type	2001
Assault	5,036
Rape/Sexual Assault	3,303
Robbery	6,810
Drug Offenses	5,761

Source: Correctional Service of Canada, 2005

Women's Issues

The objective of the Mother-Child Program is to provide mechanisms that foster and promote stability and continuity for the child in its relationship with its mother. The best interest of the child, including the physical, emotional, and spiritual well-being of the child is the primary consideration in decisions relating to participation in the Mother-Child Program. The program was piloted at the Okimaw Ohci Healing Lodge in July 1996 and full-time implementation began at Okimaw Ohci in 1997. Regional institutions will begin gradual implementation in 1998. This program is not available in maximum-security units.[3]

Prison Staff

Canadian prison guards earn an average of $48,600 per year before taxes. A recent study conducted by the union of prison guards reports that prison guards are overworked, overstressed, and underpaid. The report claims that working for the prison system is one of the most stressful jobs in the country. It also reports that working conditions have deteriorated over the past five years and nothing is being done to improve them.[4]

Parole

In 2003–2004, 7,875 prisoners were granted parole. The authority to grant parole is found in the *Corrections and Conditional Release Act* (CCRA), and the respective provincial legislation. The authority for temporary absences is found in both federal and provincial correctional legislation and is exercised by correctional authorities in provincial and territorial systems. In the federal system, the responsibility for temporary absences is shared between the National Parole Board (NPB) and the Correctional Service of Canada.

Under the CCRA, the NPB has exclusive jurisdiction and absolute discretion to grant, deny, terminate or revoke parole for inmates in federal, territorial, and many provincial institutions, except for cases under the jurisdiction of provincial parole boards. The National Parole board may also, when applicable, revoke the statutory release of an offender.

The National Parole Board relies on the CSC to prepare reports and recommendations on the cases that come before the Board. The Correctional Service of Canada supervises offenders on parole or statutory release to ensure that they adhere to the conditions of release set by the National Parole Board.

Visitation

The Commissioner of the Correctional Service of Canada ensures that general visiting is available to all inmates. But all inmates' visitors must first complete an application and informational form that provides a security check on all prospective visitors. If the prospective visitor clears the security check, which is conducted every two years, he or she is granted visitation rights. The head of a prison may authorize the refusal of a visit between an inmate and a member of the public if he believes that during the course of the visit the inmate or the visitor would jeopardize the security of the prison or the safety of an individual or plan or commit a criminal offense. In addition, every institution has private interview facilities for inmates to meet with their legal representatives. Persons eligible to visit are spouses, common-law partners, children, parents, foster parents, siblings, grandparents, and persons with whom the inmate, in the opinion of the institution head, has a close familial bond.

Private Prisons

On April 27, 2006, the Ontario government took over Canada's first large privately run prison that had opened five years earlier and housed 1,200 inmates.

It was a maximum-security institution. The Ontario government found that there was inadequate health care for the inmates, flawed security and higher reoffending rates after the privately housed inmates were released. There are no plans for instituting additional private prisons in Canada.

Notes

1. CIA, "Canada," *The World Factbook*, https://www.cia.gov/library/publications/the-world-factbook/geos/ca.html (accessed October 20, 2007).

2. Correctional Service of Canada, "Continuing to Create Choices," *Let's Talk*, http://www.csc-scc.gc.ca/text/pblct/lt-en/2007 (accessed November 20, 2008).

3. Correctional Service of Canada, "Mother-Child Program" (1997), http://www.csc-scc.gc.ca/text/prgrm/fsw/pro02-5_e.shtml.

4. Quebec's Syndicat des agents correctionnels du Canada (SACC), http://www.hour.ca/news/news.aspx?iIDArticle=327 (accessed November 20, 2008).

2

United States

T HE UNITED STATES OCCUPIES MOST OF NORTH AMERICA stretching across the continent between Mexico and Canada, and includes Hawaii in the Pacific and Alaska on the northwestern border of Canada. With 303.8 million people (July 2008 est.), the United States is the third largest nation in the world in population, behind China and India, and in area it is the third largest country by size after Russia and Canada.

Three-quarters of the population in the United States live in urban areas, and more than 40 metropolitan areas have populations over one million. Approximately 80 percent of Americans are Caucasian, 12.8 percent are African Americans, 4.4 percent are Asian or Pacific Islanders, and 0.9 percent are American Indian, Eskimo, or Aleut. Hispanic Americans make up 15.1 percent of the population.

The United States is a democratic, constitution-based federal republic headed by a president who holds executive power. The Congress, consisting of the House of Representatives and the Senate, exercises legislative power. The judicial power rests in the hands of the Supreme Court, which interprets the highest law of the land, the Constitution.[1]

As of 2008 there were 2.3 million inmates in the 1,558 state prisons and the 146 federal facilities. The incarceration rate per population in the United States is 751 per 100,000, which is the highest rate among the 21 countries included in this study. The U.S. incarceration rate is 5 to 12 times that of other industrialized countries, as well as being the highest in the world. Divided by race, 41 percent of the prisoners are African American, 34 percent are Caucasian, 19 percent are Hispanic, and 6 percent fall into the "other" category (i.e., Native American and Asian). At the end of 2006 there were 203,100 women in prison.

Among the federal prisons, 7 percent are maximum security, 20 percent are medium security and 73 percent are minimum security. Among the state prisons, 21 percent are maximum-security facilities, 32 percent are medium security, and 47 percent are minimum security.

The offenses for which the inmates were interred in prisons of different levels of security are shown below.

Table 2.2 reports the average length of sentence by the different levels of federal prison security.

The states with the highest incarceration rates are Louisiana (816), Texas (694), Mississippi (669), Oklahoma (649), and Georgia (574). The occupancy

TABLE 2.1.
United States: Offense Type by Level of Federal Prison Security (%)

Offense Type	System Wide	Minimum Security	Low Security	Medium Security	Maximum Security
Extortion, fraud, bribery	4.5	11.6	3.4	1.9	
Burglary, larceny, property offenses	5.2	5.5	5.0	4.8	
Weapons, explosives, arson	12.1	6.4	8.0	19.4	
Drug offenses	54.5	71.7	59.7	44.7	
Robbery	5.9	0.4	2.4	9.1	
Homicide, aggravated assault, kidnapping	3.3	0.2	1.5	3.7	
All others	14.5	4.2	20.0	16.4	

Source: Bureau of Prisons (BOP), 2006

TABLE 2.2.
United States: Average Length of Sentence by Level of Federal Prison Security

Sentence Length	System Wide	Minimum Security	Low Security	Medium Security	Maximum Security
<1 year	2.0	3.5	2.5	0.8	0.4
1–3 years	14.5	20.8	16.7	10.9	3.7
3–5 years	16.1	18.5	18.3	14.5	7.5
5–10 years	29.0	32.3	28.8	29.6	22.4
10–15 years	17.6	17.9	17.9	17.8	15.5
15–20 years	8.5	4.9	8.1	10.8	10.7
>20 years	9.1	2.0	7.2	13.4	18.3
Life sentence	3.2	0.1	0.5	2.2	21.5

Source: Bureau of Prisons (BOP), 2006

level for both federal and state prisons is 1,951,650 and as of 2004, they were filled to over capacity: 152 percent at the federal level and 112 percent at the state level. The recidivism rate is 40 percent.

Prison Conditions

In 1995, a survey of state and federal prisons reported that nearly one-fourth of all inmates were enrolled in some type of education program. Over 50,000 inmates were enrolled in "adult basic education" which involves classes in mathematics, reading, science and social studies. In 1996, over 37,000 inmates earned their GED, a high school equivalency degree.

About 80 percent of U.S. prisons offer the GED, and 75 percent provide basic education courses. About one-third offer college education courses. In 1996, a survey reported that 14,536 inmates received a two-year associate's degree and 232 received a bachelor's degree.

Vocational education courses are also offered. Such courses are aimed at training inmates in vocational skills that could be used to find employment after release from prison.

Data indicate that 80 percent of all inmates are given work assignments that may include institutional maintenance, laboring on a prison farm or working in a prison industry. Institutional maintenance may involve janitorial duties, food preparation, laundry, office help, barber or beauty shop, library. The inmates work on average of six hours daily and receive $1.03 to $4.38 for nonindustrial work.

Inmates are also employed in prison industries, that is, employing inmates for profitable production and services. The federal government and every state government own and operate prison industries. Their products can be sold only to governmental agencies, public organizations, tax-supported entities, or markets in other countries. In 2000, Federal Prison Industries (FPS) operated 103 factories at 68 facilities within the Federal Prison System. They offered 150 different products and services and generated $546 million in net sales and $17 million in profit. The Federal Prison Industries employed 22,000 inmates: 30 percent work in textiles, 22 percent in furniture, 18 percent in electronics, 16 percent in metals, and 14 percent in graphics and services. In 1999, the FPS paid $38 million in inmate wages. The FPS workers work an average of 7.5 hours a day and receive a daily wage ranging from $1.73 to $8.63. Fifty percent of the inmate wages are garnisheed for court fines, child support, and victim restitution.

Every state prison operates its own prison industry. The most common products are wood/furniture, metal, paper/printing, vehicle-related, and garment/textile. In 1999, state prison industries employed 56,000 inmates (7 percent of the state prison population) and generated $3 billion in sales and $67 million in profit. Inmates worked seven hours a day and the daily wage ranged from $2.26 to $6.53. The states garnished 70 percent of inmate wages for victim restitution, child support, and cost of incarceration.[2]

The HIV infection rate among prisoners is at least six times higher than in the general population.

Women's Issues

As of December 31, 2004, 104,848 women were held in state and federal prisons, up from 68,468 in 1995. Women constituted 7.0 percent of all inmates—up from 6.1 percent in 1995. In 2004, 32 percent of female inmates were incarcerated for a drug offense.[3] Ninety percent of the women in prison are single mothers. Almost all of them lose contact with their children. Women who are pregnant when they are sentenced to prison and give birth while they are incarcerated are rarely allowed to spend time with their child after birth. Only one U.S. prison, Bedford Hills in New York, allows women to keep their newborn babies with them in a special prison program. In many European prisons women are allowed to keep their babies for up to two years.

Prison Staff

As of 1995, there were a total of 339,070 employees (including custodial and security related staff, administrative staff, professional and technical staff, clerical staff, educational staff, and food services staff) in the state and federal prisons; 72 percent of the staff are men, 28 percent are women. In the state facilities there were 2.9 staff persons for every inmate and in the federal prisons there were 3.2 staff persons for every inmate.

Parole

Parole is the early supervised release of a prison inmate. Parole was first used in the United States in New York in 1876. By the turn of the century, parole was prevalent in the United States. In 1916 Congress established the U.S. Parole Commission and gave it the responsibility of evaluating and setting the release dates for federal prisoners.

At least 27 states and the District of Columbia now require violent offenders to serve 85 percent of their prison sentence before obtaining early release. Fourteen states have abolished parole board release for all offenders, with at least six other states abolishing parole board release for certain violent or felony offenders. Others still allow parole for offenders as long as they have served the required time of their sentence. An additional 13 states, like Arkansas, require violent offenders to serve a substantial portion of their minimum sentence before being eligible for release.

Visitation

Persons eligible to visit inmates are

- immediate family (e.g., mother) and close relatives (e.g., grandparents)
- embassy officials (foreign prisoners)
- members of religious and civic organizations
- attorneys
- people helping inmates transition into public or helping with family problems (clergy, prospective employers, etc.)

Each visitor has to be approved by the prison staff. Inmates have at least four hours a month of visitation time.

Private Prisons

Corrections Corporation of America (CCA) is the sixth largest corrections system in the nation, behind only the federal government and four states. CCA is the founder of the private corrections industry and is the nation's largest provide of jail, detention, and corrections services to governmental agencies. CCA has approximately 69,000 beds in 63 facilities, including 38 owned facilities, under contract for management in 19 states and the District of Columbia. The states that have the greatest number of private prisons are Texas, California, Florida, and Colorado. The company manages more than 62,000 inmates including males, females and juveniles at all security levels and does business with all three federal corrections agencies, almost half of all states, and more than a dozen local municipalities. CCA offers a variety of rehabilitation and educational programs, including basic education, life skills, and employment training and substance abuse treatment. It also provides health care (including medical, dental, and psychiatric services), food services and work and recreational programs.[4] Less than 5 percent—52,370 inmates—are housed in private facilities of U.S. prisons.

Notes

1. CIA, "United States," *The World Factbook*, https://www.cia.gov/library/publications/the-world-factbook/geos/us.html (accessed July 24, 2008).

2. Criminal Justice Institute, *The Corrections Yearbook* (New York: Criminal Justice Institute, 2000).

3. Department of Justice, Office of Justice Programs, "The Nation's Prison Population Continues Its Slow Growth," http://www.ojp.usdoj.gov/bjg/pub/press/p04pr.htm (accessed July 22, 2009).

4. Corrections Corporation of America, "About CCA" (2008), http://www.correctionscorp.com/about/ (accessed July 17, 2009).

II

LATIN AMERICA

3

Argentina

T HE FEDERAL REPUBLIC OF ARGENTINA is the second largest country in South
America, and occupies much of the southern portion of the continent
(1.1 million square miles). It has a population of 40.3 million (July 2007 est.).
It is a major agricultural producer, but is also highly industrialized, with the
vast majority of its citizens (86 percent) living in urban centers.

Argentina is a federal republic headed by a president, who is assisted by
a Council of Ministers. Legislative powers are vested in a national congress
consisting of a Senate and a Chamber of Deputies. All constitutional provisions have been repeatedly suspended and then reinstated. As of 1994, several
parts of Argentina's Constitution were revised, although the basic system of
government remained unchanged.

Argentina is a nation with a rich Spanish heritage. Spanish is the official
language and is spoken by the overwhelming majority of Argentines. Italian
and a number of Native American languages are also spoken.

Roman Catholics make up 70 percent of the population and the church
plays a major role in shaping the country's laws and policies, especially those
concerning women's issues.[1]

As of 2005 there were 462,500 prisoners in Argentina at a rate of 84 per
100,000 population. There are 2,608 or 4.2 percent female prisoners and 166
penal institutions. According to a 2005 government study, the prison population increased by 200 percent between 1998 and 2005. The large majority of
inmates in Argentinean prisons have not yet been tried. As of February 2005,
only 11 percent of the inmates have been sentenced.

Prison Conditions

Prison conditions in Argentina have been below international standards in the past and there is continued evidence that, despite policy changes in the federal government, conditions are not at an acceptable level. Policy considerations can be linked back to 1993 with the creation of the post of prison ombudsman (*Procurador Penitenciario*), who was assigned the task of monitoring the country's prisons to ensure that prisoners' rights are respected and that prison conditions meet minimum legal standards. This task is largely carried out by visitation of prisons and evaluation of the abuse complaints from inmates in order to make recommendations for reform. In 1996, two laws were passed regarding the treatment of prisoners and pretrial detainees: *ley de ejecucion de la pena privativa de la libertad,* and *reglamento general de procesados,* respectively. The laws establish a system of judicial monitoring of prison conditions and the treatment of prisoners.

While these measures can be viewed as a positive step in prison reform, negative accounts since their inception offer a different perspective of the reality of prison conditions in Argentina. For example violence in Argentina's overcrowded prisons worsened in 2005. According to a government report, three prisoners were killed every week in Buenos Aires province through March 2005, which was triple the level of violence in 2004. Guard brutality is widespread and shows no signs of diminishing.

Recent reports from Human Rights Watch and the United Nations have acknowledged improvements in the management and conditions of prisons at both the provincial and federal levels. These improvements are most likely attributed to a shift in Argentina's governing body as well as an increased interest in monitoring human rights in Argentina from external groups and countries. Even though there is a trend toward the increase in inmate rights affordability in areas such as medical care, visitation policies, and security, prisons continue to suffer from vast overcrowding and a lack of separation of inmates with violent tendencies from the general population. Such overwhelming instances greatly overshadow and will eventually consume any progress made in other areas. The fact remains that if little continues to get accomplished regarding capacity issues and commonsense security measures, the prisons will remain in a tumultuous existence until the system eventually suffers its demise from increased riots and deadly violence.

Women's Issues

The average jail term for the women prisoners is about one year and seven months. More than 70 percent of women prisoners are charged with robbery related offenses or drug possession and peddling.

A major difference in the treatment of the male and female prisoners is in the availability of education and work programs. Women rarely have the opportunity to receive an education while incarcerated either from a lack of programs available or because they must spend their time taking care of their children. Children can stay in prison with their mothers until they are four years old. After that they have to go and live with relatives or in state homes for children.

The labor training programs that are targeted at women are usually confined to traditionally female types of work: cooking, laundry, and handicrafts. These types of jobs are rarely helpful to women after they are released from prison. In fact, they can be a detriment to their ability to earn a living.

There is also significant unequal treatment of male and female inmates in terms of conjugal and family visits. Women inmates must meet strict requirements before being allowed a conjugal visit such as good behavior, proving a stable relationship (usually marriage or common-law marriage), medical examinations, and the use of contraceptives. If there are opportunities to receive conjugal visits there is often a lack of space and women must find a corner of privacy in a public space.

Women prisoners are also subjected to punishment and unequal treatment by male security guards. A woman can be placed in solitary confinement for "practicing lesbianism" or "immorality," or even after attempting suicide. Prison officials and security guards also subject women prisoners to sexual abuse, in the form of obscene sexual verbal assaults, rapes, fully nude body or vaginal searches, keeping a woman naked in her cell for days.

The lack of basic medical resources for women inmates is still another area in which they suffer undue hardships. Pregnant women receive inadequate or nonexistent prenatal care. Women are often locked into their cells overnight without the opportunity to use the bathroom, the bathrooms do not have hot water, and they are not provided with feminine hygiene products or with soaps or shampoo to wash their clothes and themselves. As a result many women suffer from vaginal infections and other vaginal health issues. While problems of poor healthcare, overcrowding, and lack of hygiene persist for male inmates as well, they have especially grave consequences for female inmates and their children.

Prison Staff

In a November 2005 report, Amnesty International recommended to the Argentinean Prison Authority that it increase the number of prison staff including those who look after the physical and psychological health of inmates, until it is sufficient to guarantee the lives and physical integrity of the inmates.[2]

Parole

Argentina is one of the few countries in South America where the life sentence is legal. Life imprisonment is the mandatory sentence when murder is committed by a relative of the victim, when it is committed by a policeman, or when it is aggravated with armed robbery or rape. Also, there have been sentences of life in cases of multiple rapes. If a person is sentenced to *prision perpetua* he could be released between 13 and 25 years of prison. If a person is sentenced to *reclusion perpetua* he will never be released. Treason also carries the life sentence.

Visitation

Spouses have visitation rights to inmates. The frequency of the visits is determined by the conduct of the prisoners; exemplary conduct permits four visits monthly and very bad conduct cancels all visits. The visits take place on Sundays and last for two hours. Certain prisoners (i.e., those who have demonstrated exemplary conduct) are granted home visits once a month that last between 12 and 24 hours.

Notes

1. U.S. Department of State, "Background Note: Argentina," *Background Notes*, http:/www.state.gov/r/pa/ei/bgn/26516.htm (accessed July 30, 2008).

2. Amnesty International, "Argentina," *Amnesty International Report 2005* (2005), http://www.unhcr.org/refworld/publisher, AMNESTY,,ARG,429b27d5 (accessed November 19, 2008).

4

Brazil

B RAZIL IS LOCATED IN EASTERN SOUTH AMERICA, and is bordered by all of the South American countries except for Ecuador and Chile. It borders the Atlantic Ocean.

With a population of 170 million (their 2000 census), Brazil is the fifth largest nation in the world and the largest in Latin America. Its six major ethnic groups make it one of the most diverse nations in the world. The ethnic groups are white, including Portuguese, German, Italian, Spanish, and Polish (53.7 percent); mixed white and black (38.5 percent); black (6 percent); and other, Japanese, Arab, Amerindian (1 percent). The main religion is Roman Catholic (73.6 percent). The languages spoken in Brazil are Portuguese (the official language), Spanish, English, and French. Major industries operating in Brazil are concentrated in transportation, communication, weapons, aircrafts, nuclear power production, and energy (Library of Congress 1997). The country is a large exporter of goods such as tin, iron, manganese, steel, sugar, coffee, cocoa, soybeans, and orange juice.

Brazil operated under military rule from 1964 to 1985 but is now a democratic nation, with a popularly elected president, a legislative branch consisting of a popularly elected Senate and Chamber of Deputies, and a judicial branch, whose eleven tribunal members are appointed by the president. Its Congress represents 15 different political parties. These governmental branches are set forth by the Constitution of 1988, or the "citizen constitution."[1]

In 2004 there were 330,642 prisoners in Brazil at a rate of 183 per 100,000 population. There are 3.3 percent, or 10,911, female prisoners and 868 penal institutions with an occupancy level of 182.7 percent. As of June 2007 there

TABLE 4.1.
Brazil: Prisoners by Offense Type (%)

Offense Type	Percent
Murder	8.9
Assault	1.0
Stealing	9.1
Robbery	23.9
Kidnapping	0.5
Drug trafficking	10.5
Association for drug trafficking	1.0
Others	9.5

Source: J. Lembruer, "Projeto Arquitetura Institucional do
   Sistem Unice de Seguranca Publica," Ministry of Justice
   FIRJAN/PNUD (Brazil, 2004).
Note: The original material was in graph form; it has been
   revised into the table presented here.

TABLE 4.2.
Brazil: Length of Prison Sentences (%)

Sentence	Percent
1 to 4 years	15.7
5 to 8 years	20.2
9 to 12 years	10.8
13 to 15 years	8.9
16 to 20 years	9.5
20 years or more	8.1

Source: J. Lembruer, "Projeto Arquitetura Institucional do Sistem Unice de Seguranca
   Publica," Ministry of Justice FIRJAN/PNUD
   (Brazil, 2004).
Note: The original material was in graph form;
   it has been revised into the table presented
   here.

were 419,551 inmates in Brazilian prisons and jails. The majority receive five
to eight year sentences.

Table 4.1 describes the types of offenses for which the inmates were interred.

Table 4.2 reports the length of the sentence.

Prison Conditions

Brazil has a continuing problem of prison violence occurring in institutions
throughout the country. According to the Human Rights Watch "World

Report 2002," much of the violence could be traced to negligence on the part of custodial staff.[2] Inmate-on-inmate violence and homicide is able to occur so frequently due to insufficient supervision of violent inmates, corrupt staff who allow contraband such as weapons and drugs into facilities, and the organization of gangs within the facilities.

The São Paulo prison system is the most notorious of all Brazilian prisons for "under-staffing, extreme overcrowding, deaths in custody, use of torture, and lack of medical and sanitation facilities."[3] Despite the multitude of problems in the São Paulo state system, the report indicates that all prisons and detention centers in Brazil suffer from widespread torture and ill treatment of inmates by staff.

Human Rights groups have cited overcrowding as being the cause of many of the brutal riots in Brazilian prisons and report that it has now (2007) reached "inhuman levels." Inmates complain of being routinely beaten and subject to methods of torture including the "parrot's perch" (involves suspension by the legs and arms from a metal bar), near asphyxiation, and electric shock.

The high levels of overcrowding combined with low levels of staffing in some of the prisons mean that the state authorities have lost control of many areas of the prisons. These areas are in effect run by small and violent groups of inmates that are a law unto themselves.

In addition to overcrowding, sanitation is very poor. Prisoners have to pay for mattresses and bedding when they first arrive.

As of 2004, more than 2,000 prisoners tested positive for HIV/AIDS.

Educational Programs

Only 17 percent of the prisoners are involved in some kind of educational activity. Considering that 80 percent of the prisoners have less than eight years of schooling, educational programs should be essential.

Working in Prison

The Penal Execution Law states that for every three days an inmate works, he or she may serve one less day of his or her sentence. But only 26 percent of the prisoners are given employment. Only 20 percent of the prisoners sentenced to fulfill their sentences in a half-open or open regime are authorized to work outside the prison wall.

Women's Issues

Even though federal law requires separate facilities for women, female prisoners are illegally placed with men or transvestites in five Brazilian states and are subjected to torture and sexual abuse. About half of the state prison systems do not have nurseries for babies or the small children of women inmates.

Women prisoners tend to have greater access to work opportunities, suffer less custodial violence, and are provided greater material support than male prisoners.

Nuns formerly administered many of the women's prisons. The São Paulo Women's Penitentiary was managed by an order of Catholic nuns until 1980. Women's prisons tend to have better levels of staffing than men's prisons, resulting in somewhat more supervision and assistance.

The São Paulo Women's Penitentiary, the largest women's prison in the country, has four main cellblocks for a total capacity of 256, although it has held up to 400 female inmates; the Women's House of Detention in Tatuapé, in the state of São Paulo, also holds over 200 inmates. The vast majority of women's prisons, however, hold fewer than 100 inmates. Many are located in buildings converted from a previous use—the João Pessoa women's prison is located in a former convent, for example—or in small annexes adjoining larger men's prisons.

Medical care is often extremely deficient in penal facilities for women. The women's prison in João Pessoa, Paraíba, for example, lacks an infirmary and a doctor; a nurse who visits three mornings a week provides medical care.

The Brazilian constitution mandates that women prisoners be permitted to keep their nursing babies during the entire lactation period. In order to implement this rule, the national prison law states that every women's prison must be equipped with a nursery for mothers and their infants. But approximately 50 percent of the state prison systems do not have nurseries for babies or small children. At the women's prison in Manaus, Amazonas state, babies can only stay with their mothers for a week because the facility is too overcrowded to permit them to remain longer. In São Paulo's 18th police precinct, women are not even allowed to spend this first week with their infants, and must give them up at the hospital.

Some facilities, on the other hand, have more flexible rules for detained mothers, allowing them to keep their infants for several years. The Women's Penitentiary in Porto Alegre, Rio Grande do Sul, is one such facility: it held 12 children ranging from babies to 5 year olds at the time we visited.[4]

Prison Staff

Police violence is one of the most internationally recognized human rights abuses in Brazil. These abuses extend to prison inmates where beatings, torture, and killings by prison guards are widespread.

In October 2006, 14 prison officials and guards were convicted of torturing 35 inmates at the juvenile detention facility in São Paulo. Two high-ranking officials were sentenced to 87 years in prison, the highest punishment ever meted out in the country for torture.

Parole

Inmates who received sentences of two or more years and have served at least one-third of their maximum sentence or have made restitution for the loss or damage caused may be granted parole by the courts. Until a final discharge is granted, parolees must sustain good behavior and remain under the supervision of an institution or an agency approved by the court.

Visitation

A prisoner has the right to at least one visit per week. They usually take place in a confined space under supervision. About a quarter of the inmates are allowed to visit privately with their wives or companions. In a few states, homosexuals may receive private visits from their mates.

Notes

1. CIA, "Brazil," *The World Factbook*, https://www.cia.gov/library/publications/the-world-factbook/geos/br.html (accessed July 30, 2008).

2. Human Rights Watch, "Americas Overview," *World Report 2002* (2002), www.hrw.org/wr2k2/americas.html (accessed November 4, 2008).

3. Ibid.

4. Human Rights Watch, "Behind Bars in Brazil" (2000), http://www.hrw.org/reports98/brazil/Brazil-12.htm#P1388_367113.

III

WESTERN EUROPE

5

Great Britain

G REAT BRITAIN IS LOCATED IN THE NORTH ATLANTIC OCEAN and lies northwest of continental Europe. Politically, Great Britain consists of England, Scotland, and Wales, as well as a number of small islands. The population is 60,943,912 (July 2008 est.). The ethnic groups are English (83.6 percent), Scottish (8.6 percent), Northern Irish (2.9 percent), Welsh (4.9 percent), black (2 percent), Indian (1.8 percent), Pakistani (1.3 percent), mixed (1.2 percent), and other (1.6 percent) (2001 census). The religions are Christian (Anglican, Roman Catholic, Presbyterian, and Methodist) (71.6 percent, 40 million), Muslim (2.7 percent), Hindu (1 percent), and other (1.6 percent). The languages spoken are English, Welsh, and Gaelic.[1]

England is a constitutional monarchy. It has an uncodified constitution that is a blend of statute law, precedent, and tradition dating back to the 1100s. Legislation may be put forth by government ministers or departments. Parliament, which is made up of the House of Lords and the House of Commons, may annul such legislation. England is a member of the European Union which entails adherence to European Community law. European Community law takes precedence over both legislation and common law. England's legal system is an adversarial one. All cases first appear in magistrates' courts, which are also known as "courts of first instance." The magistrates' courts decide if the nature of the offense is appropriate for that court and whether the parties consent to try the offense in that court. The court may decide not to try the offense in the magistrates' courts, but to commit the accused for trial in the Crown Court.

TABLE 5.1.
Great Britain: Offenses for Which Inmates Have Been Interred

	# of Inmates	% Male
Violence against another person	12,192	95.6
Arson	—	—
Rape/sexual offenses	5,305	99.6
Burglary	9,152	97.5
Robbery	7,507	95.9
Theft	4,744	90.3
Fraud and forgery	1,039	88.3
Drug offenses	10,055	86.8
Other	6,198	95.8
Offense type unknown	1,101	93.7

Source: British Prison Service

As of 2005 there were 76,030 prisoners in Great Britain at a rate of 145 per 100,000 population. Of those, 4,568 or 5.9 percent were female prisoners. There are 128 state penal institutions in Great Britain at an occupancy level of 111.4 percent and there are eleven privately contracted prisons. According to a recent study reported in the *Sunday Times* in January 2008, 10 of the 11 private prisons rank at the bottom quarter of all the penal institutions. The private prisons scored particularly badly on maintaining order and security.

As of 2002, the offenses for which inmates had been committed are shown in table 5.1.

The average length of custody excluding those sentenced to life imprisonment is 26.8 months.

Prison Conditions

There are four security categories for adults in British prisons: A, B, C, and D. Category A applies to prisoners whose escape would be highly dangerous to the public, or the police, or the security of the state, no matter how unlikely that escape might be, and for whom the aim must be to make escape impossible. Any prisoner who meets the criteria can be classed as category A. Category B applies to prisoners for whom the very highest conditions of security are not necessary, but for whom escape must be made very difficult. Category C applies to prisoners who cannot be trusted in open conditions, but who do not have the resources and will to make a determined escape attempt. Category D applies to prisoners who can reasonably be trusted in open conditions.

Young offenders may be classified as category A in the same way as adult males. Categories B, C, and D are only for adult convicted men. Pretrial remandees—unless they are category A—will not be categorized, and are usually treated as category B.[2]

In April 2002 the British Medical Association warned that limited medical resources, medical staff shortages, and poor prison management were contributing to a prison health care crisis.

Programming

A variety of prison jobs exist in England and Wales, including kitchen work, gardening, farming, and craft work, such as weaving and woodwork. Some prisoners are employed in light assembly activities or laundry and cleaning jobs. Pay levels are generally low. Prisoners are able to take National Vocational Qualifications for 48 trades and occupations. Other certification up to degree level is available.

Prisons vary in the extent to which they offer comprehensive exercise facilities. Most prisons have small prison shops and libraries. There has been movement toward allowing prisoners to wear their own clothes. There are now national guidelines on incentives and earned privileges for prisoners, which cover access to private cash, extra or improved visits, enhanced earning schemes, and community visits for eligible groups. The aim is to improve responsible behavior and increase participation in constructive activities.[3]

Women's Issues

Because of the relatively small number of women's prisons, and due to their geographical location, women tend to serve their sentences further from their homes than male prisoners. Around 55 percent of women in prison have a child under 16, 33 percent a child under 5, and 20 percent are single parents.

Every woman who is known to be pregnant is medically assessed and monitored. They may be located in a particular area of the prison dedicated to pregnant women, if the prison has such a facility. Support is provided according to individual need. Medical care is given by local maternity services and mothers give birth in a hospital with the appropriate facilities, local to the prison.

There are currently seven mother and baby units. Two, New Hall and Holloway, keep babies with their mothers up to the age of nine months. Bronzefield, Peterborough, Styal, Eastwood Park, and Askham Grange accommodate babies with their mothers up to the age of 18 months. Askham Grange is the only open prison with a mother and baby unit. Each application for admission is assessed on an individual basis by a multidisciplinary team. Every women's prison has an appointed mother and baby liaison officer, who offers help and advice to applicants.

Children are allowed to visit their mothers in prison the same way as other visitors. In some instances, prisoners are allowed extended, more relaxed visits with their children or can get permission to visit their children where they are living.[4]

Prison Staff

As of March 1995, there were 24,000 staff employed as prison officers. Of 826 prison officers recruited in 1994–1995, 659 were men, 167 were women and 24 were from ethnic minorities. New entrant prison officers undertake a training course for nine weeks. The course includes interactive skills training, physical education, control and restraints training, and learning about suicide prevention, equal opportunities, and race relations.[5]

Parole

Parole is granted on the basis of reports by prison and probation staff, on the nature of offenses, home circumstances, plans for release, behavior in prison, and so on.

For sentences before October 1, 1992 (the date the 1991 Criminal Justice Act came into effect), the arrangements for parole are as follows:

- Eligibility will be considered at the one-third point of the sentence. If parole is denied, unconditional release will occur at the two-thirds point of the sentence.
- If parole is granted, supervision will be provided by the probation service until the two-thirds point of the sentence. Any violations while on parole can result in the inmate's return to prison.

    Sentences on or after October 1, 1992: the Criminal Justice Act of 1991 introduced major changes concerning release from custody. They are as follows:
    - All prisoners other than those released on Home Detention Curfew (HDC), that is, those monitored by an electronic tag, will spend at least half their sentence in custody.

○ Those serving sentences of less than four years and who are not released on HDC will be released automatically at halfway. Those serving four years or more become eligible to be considered for release on parole at the halfway stage. Some sex offenders will be supervised until the end of their sentence term if the judge decided this when passing sentence.

○ All prisoners will be "at risk" until the very end of their sentence. If they commit a further imprisonable offense before the end of their original sentence, the court dealing with the new offense may add all or part of the outstanding sentence to any new sentence it imposes.

○ Additional Days Awarded (ADAs) are added to release dates for breaking prison rules. They will automatically set back the release date and eligibility for parole but not the date on which the full sentence ends (the Sentence Expiry Date or SED).[6]

Visitation

In addition to allowing for visitations in the prisons, Great Britain allows home leave of five days toward the end of the sentence to certain categories of prisoners to enable the prisoners to renew their contacts with their family and to prepare themselves for freedom.

Notes

1. CIA, "United Kingdom," *The World Factbook,* https://www.cia.gov/library/publications/the-world-factbook/geos/uk.html (accessed November 4, 2008).

2. HM Prison Service, *Prisoner Information Book* (2004), http://www.hmprisonservice.gov.uk/resourcecentre/publicationsdocuments/index.asp?cat=86.

3. C. Phillips, G. Cox, and K. Pease, *World Factbook of Criminal Justice Systems: England and Wales* (1995), http://www.ojp.usdoj.gov/bjs/pub/ascii/wfbcjeng.txt.

4. HM Prison Service, "Female Prisoners" (2006). http://www.hmprisonservice.gov.uk/adviceandsupport/prison_life/femaleprisoners/.

5. Phillips, Cox, and Pease, *World Factbook of Criminal Justice Systems.*

6. HM Prison Service, *Prisoner Information Book.*

6

France

FRANCE IS A REPUBLIC with executive, legislative, and judicial branches. The legal system is based on indigenous concepts of civil law. There is a judicial review of administrative but not legislative acts.

France, with a population of 60,876,136 (July 2007 est.), borders the Bay of Biscay and the English Channel, between Belgium and Spain southeast of the United Kingdom, and borders the Mediterranean Sea, between Italy and Spain. The population is composed of 90 percent French (a mix of Celtic, Latin, Germanic, and Slavic origin), 3 percent North African, and 2 percent German ethnicity. The remainder are Slavic, Indochinese, and Basque. France's population is 83 to 88 percent Roman Catholic, 2 percent Protestant, 5 to 10 percent Muslim, 4 percent unaffiliated, and 1 percent Jewish. French is the official and widely spoken language. But some speak regional dialects and languages such as Provencal, Breton, Alsatian, Corsican, Catalan, Basque, and Flemish. The largest of the Western European nations, it is also one of the four Western European trillion-dollar economies. France has a diversified industrial base and substantial agricultural resources. The government retains considerable influence over key segments of each sector, with majority ownership of railway, electricity, aircraft, and telecommunication firms.[1]

As of 2005, there were 52,908 prisoners in France at a rate of 88 per 100,000 population. Of those, 1,958 or 3.7 percent were women. There are 185 penal institutions in France with an occupancy level of 110 percent.

The offenses for which inmates have been interred are listed below.

TABLE 6.1.
France: Offenses for Which Inmates Have Been Interred

	# of Inmates	% Male
Violence against another person	6,214	94.8
Arson	—	—
Rape/sexual offenses	6,741	98.3
Burglary	—	—
Robbery	—	—
Theft	8,324	97.6
Fraud and forgery	—	—
Drug offenses	4,983	96.8
Other	5,921	96.1

Source: French Prison Service, 2005

Level of Security

Under the centralized authority of the Ministry of Justice in Paris, a network of 10 regional prison administration offices oversee 185 French prisons.[2] These prisons are divided into five categories which are based upon a mixture of security and treatment concerns for the inmates. The largest proportion of prisons are the 118 *Maisons d'arret* which are remand centers. These facilities house offenders who have either not been sentenced or who have been convicted of minor offenses with sentences less than 12 months.[3] A second type of prison is the 24 *Centres de detention* that are reserved for inmates who have sentences longer than one year and who are considered amenable to rehabilitation. The third type of prison is the *Maison Centrale*, and it is reserved for the most serious offenders. These five facilities contain inmates who are considered long-term and habitually hardened, and the emphasis in these facilities is on security rather than rehabilitation.[4] The fourth type of prison is the 28 *Centres penitentiairies*, which are mixed facilities. These prisons house inmates of varying security levels in the same building. Sections of the prison can resemble *Centres* de detention, *Centres penitentiairies*, or *Maisons centrals*. At least two sections exist in each of these prisons. The fifth type of confinement in France is the *Centres autonomes de semi-liberte* of which there are 13. These facilities are reserved for inmates with partial-release sentences. These inmates are allowed to work outside the facility and travel unaccompanied to their jobs.

In addition to the abovementioned types of facilities, some offenders are sentenced to an "open environment."[5] In this situation, judges continue to supervise the punishment protocol of the offender with a particular emphasis on treatment. Thus, the sentence typically involves rehabilitation and probation services. These sentences can occur post-release from prison, in lieu of incarceration, or concurrent with incarceration (i.e., partial-release sentences).[6]

Prison Conditions

On October 20, 2005, the International Observatory of Prison released a report that criticized prisons for being overcrowded and unsanitary.[7] The cells are filthy and rat infested and unsanitary.

Rapes were common and fistfights were daily occurrences. Many prisoners spend as much as 21 hours a day locked behind windowless steel doors in small cells. Meals are delivered to the cells and there is little opportunity to socialize with anyone but cellmates except during the twice daily exercise breaks in the prison yard. The report also stated that drug use in prison was increasing and that more and more inmates were in need of psychiatric and other medical care, but that the prison staff was unable to diagnose and treat such needs. The International Observatory of Prison reported in 2005 that France has Europe's highest suicide rate among prisoners; 115 in 2004 and 53 by mid-year 2005. Eight out of ten inmates suffer from psychiatric problems. Violence and revolt against prison authorities have increased dramatically. Between 2005 and 2006 there was a 155 percent rise in the number of riots.

As of 2004, although Muslims made up only 10 percent of the French population, they account for most of the nation's inmates. As a result of the large and increasing number of Muslim inmates, the Minister of Justice stated that new French prison guards will undergo training in how to detect signs of Islamic extremism to keep fundamentalism out of the country's penitentiaries.

Women's Issues

Female offenders are detained in 61 of the 185 prisons in accommodations that separate them from male inmates. There are also three prisons that are reserved exclusively for women. The women's sections of prisons do not have the education and employment training opportunities available to the male inmates.

French researchers describe three types of women prisoners: Classic deviants, usually serial offenders with a drug problem; women who have been the victims of violence or who are accomplices in crimes committed by their partners who are generally in prison for the first time for a serious offense (murder, child abuse, drug trafficking); and women who do not fit the pattern, professionally integrated, educated but imprisoned for a serious offense.

Prison Staff

The prison service accounts for more than 28 percent of the Ministry of Justice's budget. There are nearly 23,000 civil servants employed in the prison department of which 18,500 are prison officers and 1,400 are social workers.

Parole

Parole was introduced into the French prison system in 1985. Offenders who demonstrate some form of social rehabilitation and who have served half (two-thirds for habitual offenders) of their sentences may qualify for parole.

Visitation

In theory, all prisoners are allowed to receive visits with the consent of the French judicial system. In order to obtain an authorization to visit an inmate, the prospective visitor must contact the magistrate in charge of the prisoner's case and demonstrate his or her relationship to the inmate. The judge can refuse (without justification) to issue a visit permit to non-family members. For family members this refusal cannot exceed a month unless there is a properly documented and motivated necessity. The inmate's lawyer always has the right to communicate with his or her client.

The duration of a prison visit may vary from a half hour to two hours. The amount of visitors varies from prison to prison. An inmate cannot receive more than one visit a day.

Prisoners who have earned the right to a conjugal visit stay in decorated home-like apartments during extended visits.

Notes

1. CIA, "France," *The World Factbook,* https://www.cia.gov/library/publications/the-world-factbook/geos/fr.html. Accessed 10/20/07.

2. Le Ministere de la Justice, "The French Prison Service, Glossary," http://www.justice.gouv.fr/minister/sceri/glossgb.htm (accessed November 16, 2004).

3. Ibid.

4. HEUNI, *Criminal Justice in Europe and North America: France* (Helsinki: The European Institute of Crime Prevention and Control, 2000).

5. Ibid.

6. Ibid.

7. International Observatory of Prison (October 20, 2005).

7

Germany

THE FEDERAL REPUBLIC OF GERMANY is in Central Europe, bordered by the Baltic Sea and the North Sea, between the Netherlands and Poland, south of Denmark. It includes 137,821 square miles and is the second most populous country in Western Europe, with a population of 82 million people (2008 est.). On October 3, 1990, as a result of German unification based on a treaty between the Federal Republic of Germany (West Germany) and the communist-ruled German Democratic Republic (East Germany), Germany was reunited and Berlin became the capital of the unified Germany.

Germany is made up of 16 *Laender*, or states. The *Bundestag* (Federal German Parliament) and the *Bundesrat* (composed of members of government in the *Lander*) are the constitutional bodies with legislative authority. The federal government generally carries out executive functions in the field of homeland and foreign affairs. The federal government is headed by the federal chancellor; the federal president is the head of state and is elected for a five-year term.

The official language of Germany is German and education is conducted primarily in German. German law guarantees freedom of creed, conscience, religion, and ideological persuasion. There is no established state church. Protestants make up about 34 percent of the population, and about 34 percent of Germans are Roman Catholics.[1]

As of 2005, there were 80,413 prisoners in Germany at a rate of 97 per 100,000 population. Of those 4,101 or 4.7 percent were female prisoners. There are 237 prisons in Germany and they are at 99.9 percent occupancy level.

The offenses for which the prisoners have been committed are listed below.

TABLE 7.1.
Germany: Offenses for Which Prisoners Have Been Interred

	# of Inmates	% Male
Violence against another person	9,038	96.6
Arson	—	—
Rape/sexual offenses	2,465	96.0
Burglary	5,176	99.0
Robbery	7,641	97.8
Theft	8,627	95.1
Fraud and forgery	—	—
Drug offenses	8,791	94.9
Other	19,061	95.4

Source: German Prison Service

Prison Conditions

The prisons provide educational programs and vocational training programs. The inmates are also obligated to work at tasks which are in keeping with their physical abilities. Out of about 60,000 prisoners in Germany, between 600 and 2,000 may be HIV positive and most of these are thought to have contracted HIV, a Hepatitis B virus, or both in prison.

On August 1, 2000, almost 500 German prisoners answered a call for a coordinated one-week hunger strike protesting the conditions in the prisons. Over 28 prisons were involved in the protest. The strike publicized acts of arbitrariness, harassment, insults, psychological terror, torture, and failure to render assistance to prisoners in need of help.

German prisoners wear their own street clothes, are allowed to vote while in prison, and are generally housed in cells without observation windows. Solitary confinement in all of the prisons may not exceed 28 days. Drug users are isolated from non-drug-using prisoners.

Women's Issues

Of the 237 prisons, 7 are exclusively for women and 22 are men's prisons that have female wings.

The distribution of offenses for which the women have been incarcerated is shown below.

The majority of women (33 percent) are in prison for less than 6 months, 11 percent for 10 to 15 years, and 16 percent for life. Between 75 and 80 percent of the guards in women's prisons are men.

TABLE 7.2.
Germany: Distribution of Offenses for Which Women Have Been Interred

Offense	Percent
Property (theft and handling stolen goods, robbery, and burglary)	34
Drug	19
Fraud and forgery	23
Physical violence	9
Homicide	5
Motoring	3
Sexual offense*	1
Other	6

Source: German Prison Service
*Not prostitution since it is legal in Germany

The women prisoners have special mother and child units and in general children may remain with their mothers in these units until they are three years old.

There are programs available in the women's prisons to treat inmates with drug or alcohol addictions.

Children are allowed to visit their mothers more frequently than the specified four times a month for other relatives and the mothers are allowed to have physical contact with their children during these visits.

Prison Staff

German prison guards are career civil servants who undergo long-term training. The guards do not carry weapons.

Parole

The minimum time to be served for a sentence of life imprisonment is 15 years, after which the prisoner can apply for parole.

The German Constitutional Court has found life imprisonment without the mere possibility of parole to be antithetical to human dignity, the most fundamental concept of the present German constitution. That does not mean that every convict has to be released, but that every convict must have a realistic chance for eventual release, provided that he is not considered dangerous any more. Displays of contrition or appeals for mercy must not be made a condition for such a release. There is considerable popular opposition to the application of this ruling in the case of Red Army faction terrorists.

In cases where the convict is found to pose a clear and present danger to society, the sentence may include a provision for "preventive detention" after the actual sentence. This is not considered a punishment but a protection of the public; elements of prison discipline that are not directly security-related will be relaxed for those in preventive detention. The preventive detention is prolonged every two years until it is found that the convict is unlikely to commit further crimes. Preventive detention may last for longer than 10 years, and is used only in exceptional cases. Since 2006, it is possible for preventive detention to be ordered by a court after the original sentencing, if the dangerousness of a criminal becomes obvious only during his imprisonment.

For a person under the age of 18 (or 21, if the person is not considered to be of adult maturity, which is frequently the case) the life sentence is not applicable. The maximum punishment for a youth offender is 10 years imprisonment.

Visitation

According to the German Prison Act, prisoners have to perform work assigned to them. Education and vocational training programs are also available in the prisons.

On the whole the administration of German prisons is military-like and rule oriented.

Prisoners are given four visits a month of 50 minutes each. An exemplary prisoner may have conjugal visits of six hours a month and may request privacy. Model prisoners may leave the prison for a day to attend a birthday. They are also allowed to attend the funeral of their next of kin.

Private Prisons

As of 2005 the Serco Group was awarded a five-year contract by the Hessen Ministry of Justice to manage the Hessen prison service. This is the first private prison contract awarded in Germany. Serco will be responsible for psychological, medical, and education care as well as the building maintenance of 502 male inmates.

Notes

1. CIA, "Germany," *The World Factbook*, http://www.cia.gov/library/the-world-factbook/geos/gm.html (accessed July 24, 2008).

8

Italy

I TALY'S LOCATION IN THE CENTRAL MEDITERRANEAN strategically gives it domi-
nance in terms of southern sea and air approaches to Western Europe. Italy
has roughly 58,147,733 inhabitants (July 2007 est.) and has become a ranking industrial economy on the scale of the United Kingdom and France. It is
homogenous and approximately two-thirds of Italians live in cities. Italian is
the official language, although in some areas the use of the local language on
official documents and in education is authorized.[1] In 1992, Rome came to
the realization that it may not qualify to participate in European Union plans
for economic and monetary union later in the decade; thus it began to address
its large fiscal imbalances. As a result, the government adopted fairly stringent
budgets, abandoned its inflationary age index system, and started to scale
back its generous social welfare programs, including health care benefits.

In Italy's republic-style government, criminal laws are contained in the
penal code and many other statutes. All laws are required by the Constitution of the Italian Republic (Art. 73) to be published in the *Gazetta ufficiale
dello Stato* (the Official Gazette of the State). The country is divided into 20
administrative districts which have the power to make laws, providing they
do not conflict with the constitution. But, only the state has jurisdiction over
substantive and procedural penal law. The minister of justice is in charge of
the organization and functioning of the criminal justice system.[2]

The basic principles of the penal code and the constitution are as follows:
(a) no penalty without a law (*nulla poena sine lege*) and no crime without
a law; (b) legal responsibility rests solely on the acting individual; (c) rules
of penal law are not retroactive; (d) no one can be sentenced without a fair

trial; (e) no one can be considered guilty until a final sentence has been pronounced; (f) penalties cannot consist in treatment contrary to the sense of humanity and must tend to the rehabilitation of the offender; and (g) personal freedom is inviolable and no one shall be deprived of it except under specific provisions of the law (Constitution, art. 27). The principles of Italian penal code originated with the French Enlightenment influence. After Italy was unified in 1861, the Sardinian Penal Code of 1859 became Italy's code until a more general code was promulgated in 1889. Another criminal code was enacted on October 19, 1930 (Codice Rocco), which remains the basic statute in the field of criminal law with the exceptions of a few amendments. Amendments have broadened the alternatives to incarceration and modified the terms of pretrial detention.

The basics of Italy's justice system were determined by the Code of Criminal Procedure enacted in 1930. The code has been amended several times until a significantly different Code of Penal Procedure was developed in 1988 and came into force in 1989. The new code shifts Italy's procedural system of justice from an inquisitorial system to the more modern adversarial system.

An interesting feature of Italy's justice system is that the accused does not have the right to plead guilty to a lesser offense once he is charged with a crime. This is the principle of *obbligatorieta dell'azione penale*, which removes any discretion during the prosecution stage.

Essentially, selective enforcement does not exist because the alleged defendant must be processed through the system with the crimes for which he was charged.

The penal code divides criminal offenses into two categories: *delitti*, which are serious offenses, and *contravvenzioni*, which are less serious offenses. A distinction is also made through the severity of punishment and type of prison facility. *Delitti* crimes can carry a penalty of 15 days to 24 years imprisonment, and as much as 30 years or life imprisonment in special cases. For *contravvenzioni* crimes, the penalty is five days to three years imprisonment. Fines can amount to roughly 500,000 U.S. dollars for serious drug offenses (Penal code, art. 22, 23, 25).

A more detailed classification of the code generally classifies each crime under a specific heading: (a) crimes against the nation such as espionage, assassination of the president, terrorism; (b) crimes against public authority such as corruption, bribery, embezzlement of public property by an officer; (c) crimes against judicial authority like perjury; (d) crimes against religious feelings and against the feelings of pity toward the dead; (e) crimes that breach the peace; (f) crimes against public safety such as arson; (g) crimes against the public (forgery and counterfeiting); (h) crimes against the public economy, industry, commerce; (i) crimes against public morality like rape and prostitution; (j)

TABLE 8.1.
Italy: Offenses for Which Inmates Were Interred

	# of Inmates	% Male
Violence against another person	5,495	—
Arson	—	—
Rape/sexual offenses	637	—
Burglary	—	—
Robbery	4,741	—
Theft	1,546	—
Fraud and forgery	—	—
Drug offenses	11,874	—
Other	8,763	—

Source: Italian Prison Service

crimes against the family such as incest; (k) crimes against the person/violent crimes; and (l) crimes against property. Note that Italy's penal code considers the violent crimes of robbery, extortion, and ransom kidnapping as property crimes because their main intent is to gain property.

As of July 2006, there are 61,246 prisoners in Italy at a rate of 97 per 100,000 population. Of those, 2,657 or 4.7 percent were female prisoners.

There are 222 prisons in Italy with an occupancy level of 134.2 percent.

The offenses for which inmates were interred are listed in table 8.1.

Prison Conditions

According to the International Centre for Prison Studies (2005), there are three different types of institutions in Italy.[3] There are 163 remand institutions, 34 institutions for the execution of prison sentences, and 8 institutions for the execution of security measures. According to HEUNI, the institutions for execution of prison sentences are further subdivided into arrest centers and detention centers.[4] The institutions for the execution of security measures are further divided into prison farms, work homes, treatment and custody center, and judicial psychiatric hospitals. Marongiu offers numbers for a few of the various "security" institutions.[5] As of 1992, he states that there are two prisons reserved for offenders convicted of crimes related to "safety measures." There is also one prison reserved for prisoners with identified psychological needs. This facility focuses on providing these inmates with reeducation and rehabilitation programs. There are also four prisons aimed at rehabilitating drug offenders exclusively. Finally, Ruggiero, Ryan, and Sim offer that there is one prison that lies outside the organization structure of the others.[6] It is called a semicustody facility and is reserved for low-risk inmates sentenced to less than six months. These individuals are permitted to leave unsupervised during the day to work.

What adds further complication to the understanding of how the Italian prison system is structured is the fact that the report by HEUNI suggests that most prisons are not organized according to the legal parameters specified. Their report suggests that the Italian system lacks the financial resources to properly catalog inmates. For example, detainees under the age of 25 are supposed to be separated from the rest of the adult population and are not. Further, individuals detained prior to sentencing are not supposed to be housed with sentenced inmates, but oftentimes they are.[7]

Prisoners are required to work in the prison and are remunerated for their efforts. Under certain conditions inmates are permitted to work outside the institution.

Classes are also available for inmates to attend. For example, there are senior secondary school courses available.

Women's Issues

In 2002, 247 of the 2466 incarcerated women had children. Since 1975, mothers are allowed to keep their children with them until the child is three years old. The prison staff must provide nursery schools to help care for the children.

Prison Staff

Prison directors must be university graduates with a law degree. Prison guards are usually members of the police force but are specially selected to work in a prison and are under military discipline. In most of the prisons, there are 10 guards for every 100 prisoners.

Except for prisoners who are awaiting trial or are sentenced to solitary confinement, they are placed in groups of not less than three and not more than five in a cell.

Parole

A prisoner is eligible for parole if he or she has served at least 30 months (or 26 years for life sentences) and the time remaining on his or her sentence is less than half the total, a quarter of the total (if previously convicted), or 5 years (for sentences less than 7.5 years). In 2006, 21 inmates were granted parole.

Visitation

Inmates are allowed visits on a weekly basis. They are also allowed to communicate by telegraph, in writing, and by phone, with some restrictions.

Notes

1. CIA, "Italy," *The World Factbook,* https://www.cia.gov/library/publications/the-world-factbook/geos/it.html (accessed October 20, 2007).

2. Pietro Marongiu and Mario Biddau, *World Factbook of Criminal Justice Systems, Italy* (n.d.).

3. International Centre for Prison Studies, "Prison Brief for Italy," http://www.kcl.ac.uk/depsta/law/research/icps/worldbrief/wpb (accessed November 18, 2008).

4. HEUNI, *Criminal Justice in Europe and North America: Italy* (Helsinki: The European Institute of Crime Prevention and Control, 2000).

5. Marongiu and Biddau, *World Factbook, Italy.*

6. Vincenzo Ruggiero, Mick Ryan, and Joe Sim, *Western European Penal Systems: A Critical Anatomy* (Thousand Oaks, CA: Sage Publications, 1995).

7. HEUNI, *Criminal Justice.*

9

Sweden

THE KINGDOM OF SWEDEN is located in Northern Europe between Norway and Finland. The northeastern region borders the Gulf of Bothnia and the southeast area borders the Baltic Sea. Sweden has a population of 9,031,088 (July 2007 est.) residing in its 21 counties. The official language is Swedish, but there are small groups who speak Sami languages and Finnish. The Swedish population includes ethnic Finns and ethnic Lapps as well as immigrants from Finland, Bosnia, Iran, Norway, Denmark, Greece, and Turkey. Approximately 87 percent of Swedes are Lutheran. Others are Catholic, Orthodox, Baptist, Jewish, Buddhist, and Muslim.

The Swedish Constitution was passed on January 1, 1975. As a constitutional monarchy with a social-democratic government, Sweden consists of an executive, legislative, and judicial branch. While the king is the head of state, the position only carries ceremonial duties. The executive branch consists of a cabinet that is responsible to parliament, while the legislative branch is a unicameral parliament. The judicial branch consists of a supreme court with judges appointed by the prime minister and the cabinet.[1]

As of 2005, there were 7,332 prisoners in Sweden at a rate of 81 per 100,000 population. Of them 455, or 6.2 percent are women. There are 84 prisons with an occupancy level of 103.3 percent.

Prisons are open or closed depending on their level of security. In 2000, the average daily cost of a prisoner in a closed prison was between $222 and $334. The daily cost of inmates in open prisons was $174. Most prisons are small with a capacity of, on average, 45 beds.

The major offenses for which inmates are interred are shown below.

TABLE 9.1.
Sweden: Major Offenses for
Which Inmates Are Interred

Offense Type	2001
Property crime	3,139
Drunken driving	2,562
Violent crime	2,368
Fraud	1,139
Robbery	417
Sex crimes	270

Source: *Basic Facts about Prison and Probation Service in Sweden,* 2005 (http://www.kvv.se/templates/ KVVInfoMaterialListing4022.aspx).

Prison Conditions

Prisoners are required to work, study or attend programs, earning about $1 per hour. Ten percent of their earnings is saved for release and short-term leaves (furloughs). Over the last few years several programs have been developed for the prisoners. Since 50 percent of those sentenced to over two months imprisonment abuse drugs and/or alcohol, several programs address criminality and drug-related problems. Special units are available for those who wish to undergo treatment for drug or alcohol abuse while other units concentrate on motivating and influencing prisoners to participate in treatment programs. There are also special units for different categories of prisoners, such as young prisoners and prisoners convicted of sex crimes or driving under the influence. These wings offer programs that address specific problems for each category of prisoner.

Women's Issues

Under Section 41 of the Prisoner Treatment Act, women prisoners can have babies with them in prison. "Babies" are defined as children up to the age of 12 months. In the course of a year 15 to 20 babies may be found in a women's prison, where they usually stay for 2 or 3 months.

The number of women sentenced to prison in Sweden has increased by 50 percent in the last five years. Most of the increase, according to Swedish daily *Dagens Nyheter* (DN), is due to tougher punishment for drugs-related offenses.[2] Last year 1,165 women were sentenced to prison, compared to 778 in 2000. "The drug laws have been tightened up and the legal approach has changed," said Jerzy Sarnecki, a professor of criminology at Stockholm University. That view was confirmed by Sarnecki's fellow professor, Henrik Tham, who told DN

TABLE 9.2.
Sweden: Crimes for Which Women
Have Been Interred in Sweden

Crime	Number of Women
Drug offenses/smuggling	172
Theft	155
Traffic offenses	91
Violent crime	74
Drunken driving	64
Fraud, embezzlement	62
Public order	55
Robbery	11
Sexual offenses	5
Total	689

Source: *Basic Facts about Prison and Probation Service in Sweden,*
2005 (http://www.kvv.se/templates/KVVInfoMaterialListing4022
.aspx).

that the rapid rise should not be taken as a sign that the women of Sweden are becoming more crime-focused. "This is not an effect of any increase in the crime rate," he said. "The number of crimes committed every year has been the same every year since the beginning of the '90s. But the punishment has become longer." Around 25 percent of the 250 women in prison in Sweden today are serving time for drugs offenses, said DN. "Many have been drug abusers for a long period before they receive their first prison sentence," said Annika Bergström at Färingsö Women's Prison, one of five currently operating in Sweden.[3]

Table 9.2 above, provides a breakdown of the offenses for which women were imprisoned in 2005.

Prison Staff

The Swedish Prison and Probation Service provides employment for around 7,500 persons, most of whom work in prisons. Forty-three percent of all employees are women and just over one-fourth of the prison officers are women. Seventy-one percent of the probation officers are women.

Parole

Life imprisonment is a sentence of indeterminate length. Swedish law states that the most severe punishment is "prison for ten years or life," and so life imprisonment is in practice never shorter than ten years. However, a prisoner may apply to the government for clemency, in practice having his life sentence commuted to a set number of years, which then follows standard Swedish parole regulations. Clemency can also be granted on humanitarian grounds. The number of granted clemencies per year has been low since 1991, usually no more than one or two. Until 1991 few served more than 15 years, but since then the time spent in prison has increased and today (2007) the usual time is at least 20 to 22 years. Offenders under the age of 21 when the crime was committed cannot be sentenced to life imprisonment.

Increased criticism from prison authorities, prisoners and victims led to a revision of practices and in 2006 a new law was passed that also gave a prisoner the right to apply for a determined sentence at the Orebro Lower Court. A prisoner has to serve a minimum of 10 years in prison before applying and the set sentence can not be under 18 years, the maximum sentence allowed under Swedish law (10 years plus 4 years if one is a repeat offender and 4 years if the sentence contains other serous crimes). When granting a set sentence the court takes into account the crime, the prisoner's behavior in prison, public safety, and the chance of rehabilitation. However, some prisoners may never be released, being considered too dangerous. Of those who have been given set sentences under the new law, the sentences have ranged between 25 and 32 years.

Visitation

Under Swedish law, prisoners may receive as many visits as it is possible to arrange. In reality, limitations may be placed on this by small visiting facilities or a small number of staff. Prisoners may be visited by their children, other relatives and friends. Children under 18 may visit if the person who has custody of them gives their written permission. Children under the age of 15 must be accompanied by an adult. All visitors must be approved by the institution and are subject to checks carried out by the institution before the visit. Prisoners may also receive visits from their lawyer or probation officer, a police officer investigating a crime, a potential employer, or others whom it might be important for the prisoners to meet.

Visitors may come at special visiting times and visits last for one or two hours. Visitors who come from longer distances may visit a prisoner for up to a whole day. At open institutions prisoners may receive visits in their cell.

Notes

1. CIA, "Sweden," *The World Factbook*, https://www.cia.gov/library/publications/the-world-factbook/geos/sw.html (accessed October 20, 2007).

2. "Record Number of Women in Swedish Prisons," *The Local*, August 9, 2005, http://www.thelocal.se/1859/20050809 (accessed November 19, 2008).

3. Ibid.

IV

EASTERN EUROPE

10

Poland

POLAND IS A REPUBLIC LOCATED IN CENTRAL EUROPE, east of Germany, and west of Russia. The population is 38,518,241 (July 2007 est.). The ethnic groups in Poland are Polish (96.7 percent), German (0.4 percent), Ukrainian (0.1 percent), Belarusian (0.1 percent), and other and unspecified (2.7 percent) (2002 census). The religions are Roman Catholic (89.8 percent), Eastern Orthodox, Protestant, and other (10 percent). The national language is Polish.[1]

In 1918, Poland won its independence from a 1775 agreement between Russia, Prussia, and Austria that "partitioned" Poland.[2] During World War II, it was taken over by Germany and the Soviet Union. In 1999, Poland became a member of NATO and joined the European Union in 2004.

Since 1989, Poland has been transitioning from a communist system toward a democracy. Its government is now a parliamentary democracy, which divides power between the legislature, executive, and judicial branches. The Parliament, containing two houses—the Sejm and Senate—forms national laws, and its members are elected by citizens of Poland who are age 18 years or older. There are 49 administrative regions, or *voivodships*, in Poland. The central government appoints an individual to govern each region.[3] The Public Prosecution Office is led by the minister of justice, who also exercises the powers of attorney general.[4] The criminal justice system is comprised of four levels of courts: regional, district, appeals, and the Supreme Court. Prosecutable offenses originate from public accusations, from victims, and from private accusations. Sentences are determined by "Professional judges and lay assessors (who) together deliberate and vote on the penalty to be imposed . . . the law requires the judge and other members of the panel to rely on three factors during sentencing: (1) evidence and its evaluation, (2) the principles of science, and (3) personal experience."[5] Penal legislation is a composite of the penal code, the Code of Criminal Procedure, and the Code for the Execution of Penalties. There are three groups by which offenders are classified: felonies, misdemeanors, and transgressions. Felonies include violent crimes, while misdemeanors include crimes such as unintentional homicide, incest, and fraud. Transgressions are violations of administrative regulations and other minor offenses.

Sentencing is based on the discretion of the court, although the penal code contains suggestions as to what sentence should be imposed. The three recommendations rely on three different end goals: just deserts, general deterrence, and individual prevention. Felony offenders can receive anywhere from three years in prison to the death penalty. Misdemeanors are sanctioned by fines and incarceration.

As of 2007 there were 89, 805 inmates or 236 per 100,000 population. Of those, 2,695 or 3.1 percent were female prisoners.

There are 213 penal institutions in Poland with an occupancy level of 119.1 percent. The average sentence is two years.

The offenses for which the inmates were committed are listed below.

Prison Conditions

Overcrowding is a major problem in the Polish prisons. Staff are required to work overtime but they are not paid, instead they are given time off. Cultural rooms have been converted to cells to accommodate the overcrowding.

Most prisons do not have dining halls or toilets separate from the cells. Inmates usually end up eating all their meals in their cells, in the vicinity of the unshielded toilet.

TABLE 10.1.
Poland: Offenses for Which Prisoners Have Been Interred

	# of Inmates	% Male
Violence against another person	4,678	92.0
Arson	—	—
Rape/sexual offenses	1,894	99.8
Burglary	15,155	99.2
Robbery	12,680	98.0
Theft	—	—
Fraud and forgery	—	—
Drug offenses	—	—
Other	21,998	97.5

Source: Poland Prison Service

Prisoners serving sentences are required to work, those awaiting trial are not. But in the 1990s only about 25 percent of the inmates held jobs.

In one of the prisons (Katowice) about 80 percent of the prisoners have television in their cell.

Male prisoners are guaranteed to be able to shower once per week. Those who work can shower more often. There is hot water in all of the cells.

In Katowice Prison, the norm for prisoner's meals is 2,600 calories: for those under 24 years it is 3,000 calories. There is fruit or salad every day.

Drug use is not a major problem in the prisons. Staff report very little sexual activity among the inmates.

Women's Issues

Female prisoners are held in 28 facilities, 8 of which are exclusively for women. Inmates are segregated by gender in the other 20 facilities.

The women's prisons have maternity facilities as well as mother and baby houses, which have been reported in good condition by MacDonald. A child is allowed to stay with his or her mother up to three years of age.[6] Women are allowed to shower two times a week.

Prison Staff

Staff have monthly training by the prison service in a variety of areas. One area is on communicable diseases and drug taking. Staff have been trained to take precautions to avoid infection.

The prison service provides free medical care for staff and a holiday center that prison staff and their families can use once a year.

Parole

Life imprisonment has an indeterminate length. The prisoner sentenced to life imprisonment must serve at least 25 years in order to be eligible for parole. During sentencing, the court may choose to set a higher minimum term than 25 years. Since the reintroduction of life imprisonment in 1995, the highest minimum term is 50 years, for serial killer Krzysztof Gawlik, sentenced in 2002 for killing six people.

At present, there are more than 200 people serving life sentences in Polish prisons (in March 2006 there were 204, but the number is still growing). All are convicted for murder.

For a person under the age of 18 the life sentence is not applicable. The maximum punishment for a youth offender is 25 years.

Visitation

In the 1990s visitation rights were granted to inmates.

Notes

1. CIA, "Poland," *The World Factbook,* https://www.cia.gov/library/publications/the-world-factbook/geos/pl.html (accessed November 4, 2008).

2. Andrzej Adamski, *World Factbook of Criminal Justice Systems: Poland* (U.S. Department of Justice Bureau of Statistics), www.ojp.usoj.gov/bjs/pub/ascii/wfbcjpol.txt (accessed October 24, 2003).

3. Ibid.

4. Ibid.

5. Ibid.

6. M. MacDonald, *Prison Health Care in the Czech Republic, Hungary, and Poland* (Helsinki: The European Institute for Crime Prevention and Control, 2001).

11

Russian Federation

RUSSIA IS LOCATED IN NORTHERN ASIA, bordering the Arctic Ocean, between Europe and the northern Pacific Ocean. It has a population of 140,702,096 (July 2008 est.). The Russian Federation consists of 21 republics; 1 autonomous region; 10 autonomous areas; 6 territories; 49 regions; and 2 federal cities, Moscow and St. Petersburg. This amounts to 89 members of the Russian Federation. This vertical structure is maintained by 89 appointed presidential envoys. The ethnic groups include Russian (79.8 percent), Tatar (3.8 percent), Ukrainian (2 percent), and other (14.4 percent). The official language is Russian, with many minority languages. Religions include Russian Orthodox (15–20 percent), Muslim (10–15 percent), and other Christian (2 percent) (2006 est.).[1]

Known today as the Commonwealth of Independent States (CIS), the states have over 100 different ethnic groups located in primarily three geographic regions. Western and northern regions hold people of Slavic and European descent, Central Asian peoples live mainly in the south, and people of Mongolian and Chinese descent, the smallest group, live in the eastern region. Ethnic Russians make up over 25 million people spread throughout non-Russian republics of the former Soviet Union.

In the 1980s, the Soviet Union had few conventional prisons. About 99 percent of convicted criminals served their sentences in labor camps. These were supervised by the Main Directorate for Corrective Labor Camps (*Glavnoye upravleniye ispravitel'no-trudovykh lagerey—Gulag*), which was administered by the Ministry of Internal Affairs. The camps had four regimes of ascending severity. In the strict-regime camps, inmates worked at the most difficult jobs, usually outdoors, and received meager rations. Jobs were progressively less demanding and rations better in the three classifications of camps with more clement regimes. The system of corrective labor was viewed by Soviet authorities as successful because of the low rate of recidivism. But in the opinion of former inmates and Western observers, prisons and labor camps were notorious for their harsh conditions, arbitrary and sadistic treatment of prisoners, and flagrant abuses of human rights. In 1989 new legislation, emphasizing rehabilitation rather than punishment, was drafted to "humanize" the Gulag system. Nevertheless, few changes occurred in the conditions of most prisoners before the end of the Soviet period in 1991.

As of 2007 there were 888,100 prisoners in Russia at a rate of 574 per 100,000 population. Of those, 62,400 or 7 percent were female prisoners. About half of the inmates were incarcerated for violent offenses, more than 15 percent were alcoholics or drug addicts and 60 percent were repeat offenders. Russia has 1,040 penal institutions with an occupancy level of 79.5 percent.

Prison Conditions

Russian prisons are enclosed by a high (up to 10 m) fence equipped with security devices (alarms, video cameras, etc.), rows of barbed wire, and are patrolled by armed guards and dogs. Prisoners are kept in permanently locked mass cells (between 5 and 30 people), which they leave only to go to work, take exercise, or see a visitor.

Many of the Russian prisons are overcrowded, structurally decayed and do not receive the necessary maintenance and regular upkeep needed to operate in a safe and reliable manner. Inadequate food and medical supplies account for a high prevalence of starvation and death. As of 2006, more than 50,000 inmates had tuberculosis, 35,000 were HIV positive, and nearly 90,000 were drug addicts.

In 2005, hundreds of inmates slashed their bodies with razor blades to protest mistreatment and beatings by guards at a prison camp in the city of Lgov, 500 kilometers south of Moscow. The prison director and his two deputies were fired on July 4 after an investigation backed the inmates' claims of abuse. The unprecedented mass mutilation has outraged human rights groups and drawn attention to the nightmarish conditions that plague many Russian prisons.

Women's Issues

In Russia there are 35 correctional colonies for women, with a population of about 40,000. Ten of these institutions have accommodation for children: those in Cheliabinsk, Kemerovo Region, Khabarovsk Area, Krasnodar Area, Moscow Region, Nizhnii Novgorod, Samara, Sverdlovsk Region, Vladimir Region, and Mordovia. Children under three years of age are allowed to live with their mothers in the female colonies. As of 2003, 528 children were living in the colonies. There are also two special regime camps for repeat offenders, one of which, located in the city of Berezniaki in Perm Region, holds about 400 women.[2]

There are approximately 20,000 women in pretrial detention. There are two exclusively female investigative detention facilities, in Moscow and St. Petersburg. All the other detention facilities where women are held are mixed. The majority of the population in these prisons is male, with some cells for female prisoners.[3]

Prison Staff

The prisons are guarded by troops of the Ministry of Internal Affairs. They are generally men who have volunteered or have been summoned for military service. In total there are 465,000 members of the prison staff.

Parole

After 25 years, a criminal sentenced to life imprisonment may apply to a court for "conditional early relief" if the prisoner made no serious violations of prison rules in the last 3 years, and did not commit a serious crime during imprisonment. Parole, if granted, may carry restrictions, such as that the subject may not change residence, visit certain locations, and so forth. If the criminal commits a new offense, the court may retract the parole. If the application for parole is declined however, a new application can be filed three years later.

As life imprisonment was introduced in Russia only in 1996, prisoners will become eligible for parole only in 2021, if no changes in the law are made.

Visitation

Russian prisoners have the right of in-person visitation from family and friends. But families of prisoners in Siberia are using web cameras to communicate with their families and friends. It's the first instance in Russia but the authorities hope it will be rolled out in prisons across the country. Relatives say it's not quite the same thing as seeing a loved one in person, but it's better than a phone call or a letter.

Notes

1. CIA, "Russia," *The World Factbook,* https://www.cia.gov/library/publications/
the-world-factbook/geos/rs.html (accessed November 4, 2008).

2. Moscow Center for Prison Reform, *Structure of the Russian Penitentiary System*
(2006), http://www.prison.org/english/scheme.htm. Penal Reform International,
Penal Reform Institute: Women's Prisons in Russia (1999), http://www.penalreform
.org/english/vuln_womruss.htm.

3. Ibid.

12

Hungary

THE REPUBLIC OF HUNGARY, located in Central Europe, is a parliamentary democracy with a population of 9.9 million (July 2008 est.). Hungary is bordered by Slovakia, Ukraine, Romania, Serbia, Montenegro, Croatia, Slovenia and Austria. Approximately 92 percent of the population is Hungarian and 2 percent Roma. Hungarian is the official language. The majority of Hungarians are Roman Catholic (52 percent), while other religions that are practiced include Calvinism, Lutheranism, Greek Catholicism, and other denominations of Christianity.[1]

Until the mid-1800s, the Hungarian legal system was based on common law written in 1517. Today's criminal justice systems were developed during the late 1800s. The first code of criminal law was created in 1878 and the first criminal proceedings code was enacted in 1896. Prior to World War I, Hungary was part of the Austro-Hungarian Empire.[2] Hungary's legal system became socialist in 1948 and was based on two codes of criminal law from 1961 and 1978 and three codes of criminal procedure in 1951, 1962, and 1973. A new code of criminal procedure was enacted in 2003.[3]

Hungary's constitution was enacted in 1949 but underwent revisions in 1972, 1989, and 1997. The executive branch of the Hungarian government consists of a prime minister and the Council of Ministers, which is elected by the National Assembly. The National Assembly, whose members are also elected, is the legislative branch and elects judges. The most recent election was in April 2002. Hungary became a member of the North Atlantic Treaty Organization (NATO) in 1999 and joined the European Union in 2004.[4]

As of 2007 there were 15,720 prisoners in Hungary at a rate of 156 per 100,000 population. There are 33 prisoners with an occupancy of 145 percent. At 966, women make up 5.8 percent of the prison population. Of the 33 institutions, 14 are national prisons, 17 are county institutions and two are health institutions. Of the 14 national institutions, 8 are maximum/medium level, 5 are medium/minimum level, and 1 is a juvenile correctional facility.

The major offenses for which the prisoners are interred are aggravated assault, burglary, robbery, and motor vehicle theft.

Prison Conditions

Prisoners are required to work. Educational and vocational programs are available but prisoners are not required to attend classes.

The rules also state that inmates are entitled to at least one hour of open-air exercise per day. But because there are not enough guards to escort the inmates going from their cells to the open-air yard, this entitlement is rarely practiced.

Women's Issues

Of the 33 prisons, one holds women inmates exclusively and three have female wings in predominantly male prisons.

The major offenses for which women prisoners have been interred are shown below.

Of all the European countries, Hungary has the highest percentage of women imprisoned for property offenses at 61 percent. Hungary is distinctive also in that it has the lowest level of women imprisoned for drug offenses. Among the foreign national women prisoners 5 percent are held for drug related offenses.

Three percent of the guards working in the exclusively female prison are men.

TABLE 12.1.
Hungary: Major Offenses for Which Women Prisoners Have Been Interred

Offense Type	Percent
Property crimes (theft, handling stolen goods, robbery, and burglary)	61
Fraud and forgery	15
Homicide	12

Source: Interbational Centre for Prison Studies, Kings College, London, 2007.

As a regular practice, women inmates may keep their babies with them in special mother and child units until the baby is six months old. If permission is granted by the prison governor she may keep her baby until he or she is one year old. Children are allowed to visit their mothers once a month for 30 minutes in special visiting rooms where they may have physical contact with them.

As of 2005, 14 percent of the female inmates were enrolled in a special program for the treatment of drug or alcohol addiction.

Educational programs, including vocational education, are available for the women. But data are not available about the number of women who participate in the programs.

Prison Staff

There are 6,635 prison staff members of which 5,314 are guards and 1,320 are civil employees. A nonuniformed employee is required to have an elementary or secondary school education, a noncommanding officer must have at least a secondary school or university education, and a commanding officer must have a university education.

Parole

The earliest time inmates are eligible for parole varies from two-thirds to four-fifths of their sentence. Under extraordinary circumstances a judge may permit parole after the inmate has served half of the sentence, provided the whole sentence does not exceed three years. Parole is only an option, even if the minimum period has been passed. The decisive point is whether the aims of the punishment can be achieved without further detention, taking into account the prisoner's former behavior and internal disposition for smooth adaptation to society.

Upon the expiration of the statutory minimum, the head of the prison shall make a recommendation to the court on the question of parole. The court shall send the file to the prosecutor, who, after the perusal of the documents, shall make a motion on parole to the court and usually participates in the court hearing.

When granting parole, the court may place the prisoner under the supervision of a probation officer which entails the obligation of observing certain general rules of conduct prescribed by law, for example, he is obliged to appear before the probation officer and the police regularly, he has to report if he intends to change his dwelling place or place of work, and so forth. In addition the court may impose further behavioral rules such as prohibition from consumption of alcohol in public places, or visiting certain specified places, or the obligation of pursuing certain studies, and so forth. If the court orders parole without the supervision of a probation officer, the prisoner has only the obligation not to commit another crime.

The prosecutor has more extensive powers in relation to revocation of parole. According to the Criminal Code, parole has to be revoked if the person on parole has been sentenced to imprisonment for an offense that was committed while on parole. When other punishment has been imposed or in the case of serious breach of the rules of conduct, revocation is at the judge's discretion.

Visitation

Prisoners may receive visitors once a month. As a reward for good behavior they may be allowed to leave the prison for a weekend or other short periods of time.

Notes

1. CIA, "Hungary," *The World Factbook*, https://www.cia.gov/library/publications/the-world-factbook/geos/.hu.html (accessed July 24, 2008).

2. Ibid.

3. Erika Roth, "The Prosecution Service Function within the Hungarian Criminal Justice System," *European Journal on Criminal Policy and Research* 14, nos. 2–3 (2008).

4. CIA, "Hungary."

V
MIDDLE EAST

13

Iran

I RAN IS LOCATED IN THE MIDDLE EAST between Iraq and Pakistan. It borders the Gulf of Oman, the Persian Gulf, and the Caspian Sea. The other bordering countries are Afghanistan, Armenia, Azerbaijan, Turkey, and Turkmenistan. Iran has a population of 65,875,223 (July 2008 est.). The majority of ethnicities are Persian (51 percent), Azeri (24 percent), Gilaki and Mazandarani (8 percent), Kurd (7 percent), Arab (3 percent), Lur (2 percent), Baloch (2 percent), Turkmen (2 percent), while other groups make up the remaining 1 percent. Iran is the only country in the Middle East in which the official religion is Shiite Islam (89 percent). Of the remaining 11 percent, 9 percent are Sunni Muslim and 2 percent are Zoroastrian, Jewish, Christian, and Baha'i. The majority languages are Persian and Persian dialects (58 percent). Of the other languages, Turkic and Turkic dialects make up 26 percent; Kurdish makes up 9 percent; Luri makes up 2 percent; and Balochi, Arabic, and Turkish make up 1 percent each.[1]

Known as Persia until 1935, Iran became an Islamic republic in 1979 after the ruling Shah was forced into exile. Since that time, Iran has struggled to reconcile its conservative religious tradition with the influences of the West. Initially, conservative clerical forces stamped out westernizing liberal elements. In 1981, this conservatism displayed hostility toward the West when militant students seized the U.S. embassy in Tehran. From 1980 to 1988, Iran also fought an indecisive and bloody war with its neighbor Iraq over disputed territory.

The constitution has codified Islamic principles of government and law. Iran's president is subordinate to Ayatollah Ali Hoseini-Khamenei, the leader of the Islamic revolution since 1989. The legislative system is composed of a unicameral consultative assembly. Conservative and liberal student groups carry some weight amongst the younger population of the country. Iran's economy is a blend of central planning, village agriculture, and small-scale private enterprise. The state owns the oil industry and other large enterprises. Despite the steady income derived from Iran's rich oil industry, leaders have discussed diversification of the oil industry and other market forms.

As of 2006, the prison population in Iran was 150,321 at a rate of 212 per 100,000 population. Of those, 3.5 percent were female prisoners.

There are 184 prisons in Iran with an occupancy level of 243.1 percent.

A large proportion of the prisoners are political and depending on the theological classification of the type of political crime committed, the prisoners are categorized as being either a polytheist, evil, corrupt, or hypocrite. Based on their position in the classification, their sentences range from prison with tongue-lashing to prison with torture only and prison with torture and execution.

Once in prison, these inmates are differentially categorized based upon their willingness to confess and repent. Offenders who are particularly unrepentant are sent to the "casket," which is a small space divided by wood panels and is the size of a grave. Thus, individuals in the "casket" cannot stand and can only sit up or lie as if in a casket. Inmates spend from two weeks to two months in this small cell, leaving only to go to the restroom. If the prisoner remains unrepentant, he is often moved to the "resurrection" cell. These cells have multiple people and involve daily torture and intense interrogation while chained to a wall. The interrogation involves questions about the Islamic regime, the war with Iraq, and their position toward the United States, the Soviet Union, and Israel. They are also asked their opinion about the way they are treated in prison and whether or not they are ready to repent. The most famous "resurrections" are those of the Jahlahzar prison in Tehran, administered until the direction of the famous prison guard who created the concept of "resurrections," known to prisoners as Hajj Daoud.

Over half of the prisoners in Iran are confined for drug-related offenses, and it is unclear if they are subjected to the same conditions as the political prisoners or if they are confined in different facilities and treated differently.[2]

Prison Conditions

Torture is widespread in Iranian prisons. Iran's constitution specifically outlaws torture, but human rights groups say security forces routinely use it to extract confessions.

The prisons are infested with cockroaches and biting insects and inmates who do not have beds sleep on the filth-mired floors. The food is virtually inedible, contaminated with rodent droppings and crawling with cockroaches.

Women's Issues

Most prisoners were charged with drug offenses, passing bad checks, or fraud. With the Islamic revolution and the imposition of Islamic law, women now are imprisoned for acts that were not criminal offenses before, such as un-Islamic dress or sexual relations outside of marriage.

In one of the largest prisons in Iran, there are special accommodations for pregnant women and new mothers. Newborns are allowed to be raised by their mothers in the prison until they are three years told. After the child is three years old, he or she is usually sent to a state-run welfare home.

There are two public telephones in the corridors and inmates are allowed to use them for 10 minutes a day. There is an open-air yard where women can play netball and an indoor gym. A library and a small snack shop are also part of the facilities. Literacy classes are available as well as instruction in carpet weaving.

Prison Staff

The staff of the women's section of the prison is almost entirely men. They have not received any training in the issues of criminal justice or the administration of prisons. Most of the staff are illiterate.

Parole

As of 1993, prisoners may ask for parole after completing one-third of their sentence.

Visitation

Political prisoners do not have visitation rights.

Notes

1. CIA, "Iran," *The World Factbook,* https://www.cia.gov/library/publications/the -world-factbook/geos/ir.html (accessed on July 30, 2008).

2. International Centre for Prison Studies, "Prison Brief for Iran," http://www.kcl .ac.uk/depsta/rel/icps/worldbrief/middle_east_records.php?code=96 (accessed February 3, 2005).

14

Israel

ISRAEL, A COUNTRY with a population of 7.1 million, about one-fifth of whom are Arabs, is located between Egypt and Lebanon bordering the Mediterranean Sea. The ethnicities are Jewish (76.4 percent) and non-Jewish (mostly Arab, 23.6 percent) (2004 est.). The major religions are Judaism (76.4 percent), Islam (16 percent), Christianity (2.1 percent), Druze (1.6 percent), and unspecified (3.9 percent) (2004 est.). Hebrew is the official language; however, Arabic is used officially for the Arab minority and English is the most commonly used foreign language.[1]

Modern Israel was established in 1947 when the United Nations voted for the partition of Palestine into the Kingdom of Jordan and the State of Israel. Israel is a democratic society and characterized by ethnic pluralism.

Although Israel lacks a formal constitution, over the years, the country has enacted a series of Basic Laws. The most far reaching are the Basic Law on Human Dignity and Liberty and the Basic Law on Freedom of Occupation, enacted in 1992. Israeli criminal and penal law derives from major statutes passed by the parliament, known as the Knesset, which is the supreme legislative body of the State of Israel. The criminal code was developed in 1965 and the penal law was written in 1977. The latter replaced the Criminal Code Ordinance of 1936, a comprehensive code based on English common law.

Each year, the Israeli National Police collects and publishes the *Israel National Police, Annual Report*. Crime statistics can also be found in the *Statistical Abstract of Israel*. Crimes are classified according to 11 major offenses. The major offenses are also divided into subcategories. The 11 major offenses are: offenses against human lives, human bodily harm, offenses against morals, sex offenses, offenses against public order, offenses against property, drug offenses, fraud offenses, economic offenses, administrative offenses, and licensing offenses.

There has been an increase in the number of murders, which police believe is related to the increased warring between rival drug gangs. But Israel's murder rate remains one of the lowest in the industrialized world.[2] The death penalty can be imposed for two types of offenses: offenses against humanity and against the Jewish people committed by the Nazis and their abettors, and for treason in wartime. In actuality, the death penalty only has been used in rare instances.

Israel's incarceration rate is higher than most of Europe, but less than the United States. As of 2004 there were 13,603 prisoners in Israel for a population rate of 209. Of those, 313 or 2.3 percent were female prisoners. According to the Israel Prison Service (IPS) Annual Report of 1996, 50 percent of incarcerated criminals abuse drugs.[3]

There are 24 penal institutions in Israel with an occupancy level of 97.2 percent.

As of 1992, five of the prisons are considered maximum security, two minimum security, one for juveniles, one for women, and two have mixed categories. The high-security prisons are distinguished from the minimum-security prisons by having more secured perimeters (i.e., electrified fencing). In addition to the prisons being classified by security level, the prisoners are also categorized. The IPS has a Diagnostic and Classification Center attached to its Central Detention Facility where all inmates are processed prior to being placed in a prison. The prisoners are divided into 30 categories ranging from criminals, dangerous, white collar, high-risk escapees, women, and solitaries.

The offenses for which the inmates have been committed are listed below.

TABLE 14.1.
Israel: Offenses for Which Prisoners Have Been Interred

	# of Inmates	% Male
Violence against another person	4,054	93.9
Arson	—	—
Rape/sexual offenses	2,016	99.6
Burglary	2,220	94.8
Robbery	2,535	94.7
Theft	1,258	90.2
Fraud and forgery	551	80.2
Drug offenses	1,840	90.9
Other	3,604	94.0

Source: Israel Prison Service

Prison Conditions

IPS is responsible for securing the Israeli prisons. There are 3,325 employees in the IPS. About 68 percent deal with the security of the inmates, 23 percent as administrative staff and 9 percent deal with the welfare and care of the inmates. The ranks of the IPS are similar to those used by the Israeli National Police.

In some of the prisons educational programs are available that allow prisoners to complete their elementary or secondary education. Also, vocational training is available in carpentry, bookbinding, printing, tailoring, and shoe-making. Prisoners also have opportunities for employment in small-scale enterprises operated by the prison service or by private entrepreneurs.

Women's Issues

There is one women's prison in Israel, Neve Tirza. Of the 300-some inmates, 70 percent are drug addicts, mainly heroin.

Women inmates who bear children while they are in prison are permitted to keep their children in the facility until the child reaches two years of age.

A 2004 Human Rights report claims that arbitrary punishments are increasing and becoming harsher.[4] A new method of punishing the women is by imposing fines on them that are taken out of their prison canteen account. The report asserts that the women have to buy additional food in order to complement the poor prison diets and other basics and therefore the fines are a serious punishment. The women are also often put into solitary confinement in very small and dirty cells. They are prevented from receiving family visits. The reports also states that medical care is insufficient and unprofessional.

Prison Staff

The IPS is responsible for maintaining civilian prisons in Israel, as well as some security prisons containing Palestinian detainees. It is under the jurisdiction of the Internal Security Ministry. There are three special units within the IPS. Masada specializes in suppression of prisoner uprisings, especially in prisons containing Palestinian detainees. It consists mainly of special forces veterans from the Israeli Defense Forces.

A second special unit is Nahshon whose responsibilities involve searches, silencing disturbances and guarding IPS staff.

The third special unit is Yamar Dror which specializes in searches for narcotics. The ranks in the IPS are sailors, noncommissioned officers, and officers, from second lieutenant to lieutenant general.

Parole

Furloughs are granted for good behavior. A temporary parole is often allowed for nonsecurity prisoners who have served one-third of their sentence. After completing two-thirds of their sentences such prisoners could earn permanent parole for good behavior. Although parole is not extended to inmates convicted of security offenses, the president has the authority to grant pardons and, on occasion, group amnesties have been offered to security prisoners.

Visitation

Nonsecurity prisoners have visitation rights of one visit per month. They also have the right to use the telephone. Hamas and Hizbullah prisoners do not have visitation rights.

Private Prisons

Because Israel suffers from a perennial shortage of prison space the IPS decided in 2005 to contract for the building of an 800-person prison. For example in 2005, 680 inmates were sleeping on the floors and IPS representatives believe if measures are not taken, 2,600 inmates will not have beds in 2007. In testifying before the Law and Justice Committee of the Israeli Knesset in August 2005, IPS representatives stated that Israel's prison conditions rank last in the developed nations.[5]

Notes

1. CIA, "Israel," *The World Factbook,* https://www.cia.gov/library/publications/the-world-factbook/geos/is.html (accessed November 4, 2008).

2. Abe Selig, "Israel's Murder Rate among Lowest in the World," *Jerusalem Post,* June 26, 2008.

3. Israeli Prison Service, *Annual Report 1996,* http://www.mfa.gov.il/mfa/mfaarchives/1990_1999/1998/7/israel%20p (Accessed November 19, 2008).

4. *Human Rights Report 2004.*

5. Europe Media Monitor, *News Explorer,* August 30, 2005.

15

Egypt

E GYPT IS LOCATED IN NORTHERN AFRICA on the Mediterranean Sea, between Libya and the Gaza Strip, and the Red Sea north of Sudan. It is the most populous country in Africa after Nigeria. In 2008, the population of Egypt was estimated to be 81,713,520. Slightly more than half of Egyptians, 56 percent, live in rural regions.

Egypt is a republic with power concentrated in the head of state, the president. The prime minister is appointed by the president and serves as the head of the government. The legislature is bicameral and consists of the People's Assembly and the Advisory Council (functions only in a consultative role).

Nearly the entire population of Egypt speaks Arabic, but only well-educated people easily understand standard Arabic. Colloquial Egyptian Arabic is the language of daily conversation. English and French are common second languages among educated Egyptians.

Islam is the official religion of Egypt, and its legal statutes are the primary source of the country's civil law. Nine out of ten Egyptians are Muslims; almost all of the remainder are Coptic Christians, the largest Christian minority in the Middle East.[1]

As of 2005 there were 61,845 prisoners in Egypt at a rate of 87 per 100,000 population. Of those 2,659 or 4.3 percent were female prisoners.

There are 43 penal institutions in Egypt and they are divided into four categories: penitentiaries, general prisons, district jails, and juvenile reformatories. Individuals are assigned to these institutions based upon the length of their sentence. District jails are reserved for those serving up to three months.

Those serving more than three months are sentenced to the general prison houses. Offenders convicted of heavy sentences are sent to penitentiaries where they are required to work in hard labor.

The major offenses for which prisoners are interred are drug trafficking and use, corruption, and embezzlement.

Prison Conditions

Overcrowding is a major problem in Egyptian prisons. The prisons are also old, have inadequate light, ventilation, and living space. Many of the cells have no toilets or running water and no mattresses.

A report issued by the Egyptian Office of Human Rights (EOHR) describes an increased use of torture and ill treatment of inmates; deteriorating living conditions (i.e., malnutrition and pollution of drinking water); and denial of access to education. Only 0.4 percent of all prisoners are engaged in secondary education programs, and 0.7 percent in university study.[2]

Amnesty International reports that inmates are often denied sufficient opportunities to communicate with their families or to have confidential meetings with their legal advisors. Lawyers are not given the opportunity to speak to their clients in private; all meetings are monitored by a prison guard, and prisoners are regularly ill-treated en route to and from the visitors and have to go there blindfolded.[3]

Amnesty International also urges the Egyptian government to stop torture and inhuman and degrading treatment of the prisoners. Prisoners should be provided with at least the basic necessities and be given unrestricted access to appropriate medical care.[4]

Women's Issues

Female inmates are segregated from male inmates and are allowed to bring infant children with them to prison. But there are no facilities for pregnant women and no gynecologists in the women's prisons.

Many of the women inmates have been forced into prostitution by male family members or into drug dealing.

Women inmates are forced to disrobe before male prison employees. The prison staff are almost entirely men. The employees who are women hold positions at the bottom of the prison hierarchy. And any signs of sympathy that they display toward the women inmates are grounds for punishment.

Prison Staff

Amnesty International reports that security officers routinely torture, sexually abuse, and generally ill-treat prisoners.[5]

Parole

As of July 2004, inmates may apply for parole. An examination committee composed of members of the prisons sector hold monthly reviews with inmates and examine their files with the aim of releasing those who meet the conditions of good behavior.

Visitation

As of September 2004, the Ministry of Interior has ratified a decision that allows sentenced prisoners who behave well to receive their families. Some prisoners are also permitted to leave the prison for 48 hours and visit with their families.

Notes

1. CIA, "Egypt," *The World Factbook,* https://www.cia.gov/library/publications/the-world-factbook/geos/eg.html (accessed November 4, 2008).

2. U.S. Department of State, "Torture: An Unchecked Phenomena," *Egyptian Organization for Human Rights (EOHR),* http://www.state.gov/g/drl/rls/hrrpt/2004/41720.htm (accessed November 19, 2008).

3. Amnesty International, "AI Index," MDE, *Publications on Egypt, 1995–1998* (December 23, 1998).

4. Ibid.

5. Ibid.

VI
AFRICA

16

Nigeria

N IGERIA IS LOCATED IN WESTERN AFRICA. It borders the Gulf of Guinea and is between Cameroon and Benin. Nigeria has a population of 135,031,164 with more than 250 ethnic groups. The majority groups of Hausa and Fulani make up 29 percent, followed by Yoruba (21 percent), Igbo (Ibo) (18 percent), Ijaw (10 percent), Kanuri (4 percent), Ibibio (3.5 percent), and Tiv (2.5 percent). The majority of the people in Nigeria are Muslim (50 percent), Christian (40 percent), and indigenous (10 percent). English is the official language, although Hausa, Yoruba, Iagbo (Ibo), and Fulani are also spoken.[1]

The British gained control over Nigeria in 1900 and its laws—including the criminal and penal code—were based largely on those in England. Differences between Islamic law and English criminal law were problematic, since many of the inhabitants of northern Nigeria were Muslims. A new penal code, developed in 1959, was based on the Sudanese penal code, because Sudan's Muslim laws were similar to the local code of the Muslims in northern Nigeria.[2]

After Nigeria gained its independence in 1960, the criminal code and penal code were amended many times to more closely reflect the values and customs of the Nigerian people. Although these laws reflect much of the Nigerian culture, Nigeria generally operates a tripartite system of criminal justice where the criminal code (including criminal procedure) is largely based on English common law and legal practice, the penal code is based on the local Maliki law and the Muslim system of law and justice, and customary law is based on immemorial customs and traditions. In some parts of Nigeria the native laws and customs are written, and in some, they are unwritten.

As of 2004, there were 39,153 prisoners in Nigeria at a rate of 31 per 100,000 population. Of those, 744 or 1.9 percent were women. Some two-thirds of the inmates have not been convicted, many of them have to wait for years, some as long as 10, before their case comes to court.

In January 2008, the government announced that all inmates who have spent 3 to 10 years awaiting trial will have their case reviewed for immediate release. Those who had already spent more time in prison than their prospective sentence will be let out.

There are 147 penal institutions in Nigeria with an occupancy level of 92 percent.

These institutions are divided into five categories based on levels of security. The first three categories are comprised of maximum-, medium-, and minimum-security prisons. The largest proportion of these institutions are either medium- or minimum-security, as there is only one maximum-security prison in Nigeria. The largest prison complex in Nigeria, which has both medium- and maximum-security branches, is Kirikiri Prison, in Lagos.

Outside the traditional prisons, there are also "open" prisons in many metropolitan cities of Nigeria. While we are not sure as to the Nigerian definition of open prisons, they are commonly distinguished from traditional prisons in several ways. These prisons normally do not have extensive security around the parameter, guards do not carry weapons, and prisoners are permitted to engage in open communication throughout the normal course of the day.[3] Further, rehabilitation is the prevailing goal behind these institutions.

In addition to open prisons, an alternative to the traditional prisons are Borstal homes. They are categorized as between a minimum- and maximum-security prison and are generally reserved for younger offenders who have not committed very serious crimes. In addition to the five confinement institutions comprising the penitentiary system, there are also county lock-ups in Nigeria. As of 1992, there were 242 county lock-ups.[4]

The major offenses for which prisoners are interred are property offenses which include stealing, robbery, forgery, motor theft, fraud, bribery, and pick-pocketing.

Prison Conditions

Many of the inmates are crammed into massively overcrowded, dilapidated cells in old prisons. Many of the cells have no beds or mattresses. The inmates sleep on concrete floors. In cells where there are beds, many inmates sleep two to a bed. Toilets, often little more than holes in the floor are usually overflowing by the end of the day. In addition to overpopulation, lack of food is a major problem. Some inmates rely on their families to bring them food.

Children under the age of 18 are held together with adults in four of Nigeria's largest prisons

Some of the prisons offer educational or work opportunities to a limited number of prisoners, but in those prisons that do offer programs there are not a sufficient number of books, instructional supplies, and vocational training materials.

All of the prisons have medical staff and welfare officials but according to Amnesty International inmates reported that access to staff or medication was available only to those who could afford bribes.

Women's Issues

Three hundred babies were born in Nigerian prisons by female inmates between 1999 and 2007.

Overcrowding is as much a problem in the women's prisons as it is in the men's facilities. For example, in one of the women's prisons, 18 women live in two cells. They sleep on iron beds stacked one atop another, some without mattresses. Many of the bathrooms do not have running water. There are no sanitary napkins. Mosquitoes are everywhere and there are no bed nets. Many suffer from malaria.

Prison Staff

According to Amnesty International, prison staff work long and stressful hours for low wages that are often paid late. Their poor pay often leads to petty extortion of inmates, and staff shortages create security risks for both staff and inmates.

Parole

On June 19, 2008, a bill to establish a national parole was introduced into the national legislature. If the bill passes not all offenders will spend their full term of sentence in prison. It would allow for release of inmates on grounds of good behavior.

Visitation

Government policy makes it very difficult for inmates to have visits. Some prisoners, for example, are transferred to prisons that are farthest from their homes in order to isolate them from their families and friends.

Notes

1. CIA, "Nigeria," *The World Factbook,* https://www.cia.gov/library/publications/the-world-factbook/geos/ni.html (accessed October 20, 2007).

2. Obi Ebbe, *World Factbook of Criminal Justice Systems, Nigeria* (1992), 1.

3. Christoph Maeder, "Everyday Routine, Social Structure and Sociological Theory: Using Ethnographic Semantics for Research on Prisons," *Forum: Qualitative Social Research* 3, no. 1 (January 2002).

4. Ebbe, *World Factbook, Nigeria.*

17

South Africa

B EFORE AUGUST 1993, the country was a racial oligarchy in which apartheid controlled every aspect of life on the basis of racial classification. South Africa is currently a nonracial democracy of roughly 44 million people (July 2007 est.), the fifth largest in Africa. The population is comprised of 79 percent black, 9.6 percent white, 8.9 percent colored, and 2.5 percent Indian (2001 Census). The main religion is Christianity (79.7 percent) and includes most whites, coloreds, and about 60 percent of blacks and 40 percent of Indians. The remaining religions include Muslim (1.5 percent), other (2.3 percent), and the rest traditional and animistic (16.5 percent). Major languages are IsiZulu (23.8 percent), IsiXhosa (17.6 percent), Afrikaans (13.3 percent), Sepedi (9.4 percent), English (8.2 percent), Setswana (8.2 percent), and Sesotho (7.9 percent).[1]

With the fall of apartheid, criminal activity became very visible. The rapid transition to a democratic government produced conditions that are favorable to organized crime groups. Rapid transition is usually accompanied by reforms of the security forces and replacement of personnel with new individuals often not equipped to take on the new responsibilities. Similarly, judicial institutions now are responsible for protecting individual freedoms instead of repressing any opposition. Outdated laws and weak judicial and police institutions provide the right atmosphere for criminal activity to flourish.

Crimes are referred to as either "crimes" or "offenses" and generally people use the term "crime" to refer to the more serious forms of criminal conduct such as murder, theft, and rape, and the term "offense" to refer to less serious conduct (like misdemeanors in the United States) as contraventions of municipal bylaws.[2]

As of 2005, there were 156,175 prisoners in South Africa for a rate of 344 per 100,000 population. Of those, 3,436 or 2.2 percent were female.

There are 224 penal institutions with an occupancy level of 164.1 percent.

The prisons are divided into four categories based upon level of security.[3] They include: minimum-security, medium-security, maximum-security, and closed-maximum prisons. The prisons receive these designations based upon the security level of the perimeter and the amount of free movement granted to the inmates. Not only are prisons classified, but offenders are also classified according to the risks they pose to fellow prisoners, personnel, and the community at large. Thus, within any level of prison, there may be wings that house inmates presenting greater or lesser threats than the security ranking of the facility intends. One frequent occurrence due to overcrowding is that offenders intended for maximum-security prisons are housed in special wings in medium-security prisons.[4]

Offenses for which the inmates are committed are listed below.

Prison Conditions

Many prisons throughout South Africa operate at less than adequate standards. Not only are inmates forced to endure significant time in cells without the option of work or recreation, but the cells are often unsanitary and in disrepair. Older prisons have documented structural issues, such as broken windows, and faulty plumbing and electrical writing. Some communal cells are crowded to the point where inmates are either forced to sleep side by side

TABLE 17.1.
South Africa: Offenses for Which Inmates Are Interred

	# of Inmates	% Male
Violence against another person	67,743	—
Arson	—	—
Rape/sexual offenses	17,556	—
Burglary	—	—
Robbery	—	—
Theft	—	—
Fraud and forgery	—	—
Drug offenses	—	—
Other	—	—

Source: South Africa Department of Correctional Services

or on the floor. There are reports of widespread beatings of inmates in the mixed juvenile/adult cells. The Office of the Inspecting Judge reported that fellow prisoners raped an estimated 70 to 80 percent of arrested suspects. Nutrition has also been a source of complaints from inmates. Meals of miele pap, ground fish meal, and bread slices lack the adequate sustenance and caloric intake needs of most inmates.[5]

Women's Issues

The South African prison system allows women with children of up to two years of age, and in some cases up to four years, to keep the children with them in prison. If the mothers are required to work, their babies were cared for during the mothers' work hours in moderately well-appointed nurseries by assigned prisoners. Babies born in prison do not have that fact noted on their birth registration document.

Women are at a disadvantage compared with their male counterparts in prisons in several areas. Where there is work, women are usually required to perform what is described as "typically women's work," such as laundry or sewing. There is hardly any vocational training for women. According to government statistics, as of June 30, 1991, out of 2,581 prisoners receiving vocational training nationwide, only nine were female. They were training as hairdressers. In one prison complex, in Durban, the female prison was the only institution without phones for inmates' use.[6]

Prison Staff

Many inmates in South African prisons are expected to be HIV positive, or have another type of sexually transmitted disease (STD) upon entering prison.

- 30 percent estimated to be HIV positive in South African prisons
- 90 percent of South African prison deaths were from AIDS[7]

Adequate staffing levels in South African prisons have been a problem for maintaining security in facilities. In some cases, members of the Prison Service Reserve Force, which are predominantly retirees and military reservists, have been called in to assist prison staff in daily operations.

The staffing shortage presents a particular problem due to the fact that prison gangs are large and widespread in South Africa. Even though these gangs do not usually flourish outside of prisons, they have existed for over

100 years.[8] The largest South African prison gangs are the 26s and 28s, quite possibly named for their initial number of permanent members. These gangs have been known to fight each other and commit other violent acts, although most of it takes place after in-depth planning. Prison gangs have divisions of leaders and follow a hierarchical structure, and rival gangs have been observed to peacefully coexist at times with each other.

Parole

Inmates who have served more than half their sentence and have a record of good behavior may be released on parole. The parolees are supervised so as to achieve their successful reintegration into the community, to combat recidivism, and to protect the community. The supervision of parolees can range from very confined to their homes to monthly telephone monitoring. If the behavior of a prisoner in parole justifies it, the supervisory measures are relaxed.

Visitation

Visitation for sentenced inmates depends on the category in which they are classified. Visits can be limited to two times per month for twenty minutes. Some of the visits can be exchanged for telephone calls. Access to incoming or outgoing mail is unlimited but is subject to censorship.

Private Prisons

Privatizing prisons was first considered an option by the South African government in 1994, and was later implemented through the passage of the Correctional Services Act of 1998. Through this act, the government was authorized to provide contracts on prison services to the private sector. The only area that was not eligible for private bids was community corrections, which is generally an area that private firms fiercely compete for in the United States and United Kingdom.[9] The entire process of privatization is monitored by an independent agency, the Judicial Inspectorate.

Notes

1. CIA, "South Africa," *The World Factbook*, https://www.cia.gov/library/publications/the-world-factbook/geos/sf.html (accessed October 20, 2007).

2. C. R. Snyman, *Criminal Law* (Durban: Butterworths, 1984).

3. Department of Correctional Service, "Safety and Security," *Offender Management,* http://www-dcs.pwv.gov.za/OffenderManagement/Safetyandsecurity.htm (accessed January 26, 2005).

4. Ibid.

5. Office of the Judicial Inspectorate (2001).

6. Human Rights Watch, *Human Rights Watch World Report 2002: Special Issues and Campaigns: Prisons* (2002), http://hrw.org/reports/1994/southafrica/13.htm.

7. Chester N. Morris, Barry Levine, Gail Goodrich, Nkandu Luo, and Jeffrey Ashley, "Three-Country Assessment of Alcohol-HIV Related Policy and Programmematic Responses in Africa," *African Journal of Drug & Alcohol Studies* 5, no. 2 (2006).

8. N. Haysom, *Towards an Understanding of Prison Gangs* (Cape Town: University of Cape Town, 1981).

9. K. C. Goyer, *Prison Privatisation in South Africa: Issues, Challenges and Opportunities,* Monograph 64 (Institute for Security Studies, 2002), http://www.pmg.org.za/minutes/20020311-institute-security-studies (accessed December 1, 2008).

VII

ASIA

18

India

INDIA IS LOCATED IN SOUTHERN ASIA, bordering the Arabian Sea and the Bay of Bengal, between Burma and Pakistan. It is a pluralistic and diverse culture with 1,129.8 million people. Hindus represent 80.5 percent of the population; 13.4 percent are Muslims; 2.3 percent are Christians; and the remaining are Sikhs, Buddhists, and a mixture of other religions. Hindi is the national language and primary tongue of 30 percent of the people while English has associate status but is the most important language for national, political, and commercial communication. There are 14 other official languages as well.[1]

India became a sovereign democratic republic in January 1950 after attaining independence from Britain in 1947. A quasi-federal system of government, India has a president who acts as head of state. A prime minister advises the president. The country's 25 states are each headed by a governor appointed by the Union government. There are also seven Union Territories which are directly administered by the Union government through its officials.

The criminal justice system in India is based on the British system. It has four subsystems, those being the legislature (Parliament), enforcement (police), adjudication (courts), and corrections (prisons, community facilities). India's penal code originated in 1860 and was largely influenced by English criminal law, followed by the adoption of a criminal code in 1861. However, the criminal code was repealed and replaced by a new code in 1974. Criminal offenses are divided into two categories: cognizable crimes and noncognizable crimes. The former are the more serious crimes, for which a police officer does not need a warrant to make an arrest. The latter are more trivial and a warrant is needed for arrest.

As of 2006, there were 358,368 prisoners in India for a rate of 32 per 100,000 population. Of those, 13,986 or 3.9 percent were female prisoners.

Although 84 percent of India's population is Hindu and 13 percent are Muslim, (2.4 percent are Christian), a much higher percentage of Muslims are inmates of India's prisons. For example, in Maharashtra, Muslims account for 10.6 percent of the population and 32.4 percent of the prison population. In Gujarat, Muslims account for 9.06 percent of the population, and 25 percent of the prison inmates. There is no breakdown on the types of offenses for which Muslims are incarcerated, but the majority are not imprisoned for terrorism. One possible explanation is that in urban areas, 44 percent living at the poverty level are Muslims compared to 28 percent at the national level.

There are 1,328 prisons in India with an occupancy level of 145.4 percent.

These penal institutions are divided into 109 central prisons, 284 district prisons, 849 subprisons, 27 open prisons, 14 exclusive prisons for women prisoners, 12 Borstal schools, 7 juvenile camps, and 26 special prisons. The prison system in India, like China and Australia, is decentralized. Thus, prisoners are categorized and punished differently depending on the state within which they are sentenced. According to Raghavan, Tamil Nadu is a typical state.[2] Here, there are five categories of prisons. Women, juveniles, and males serving less than one month serve their sentences in prisons reserved exclusively for them. The other two types of prisons are for males serving more than one month. The difference between the two prisons is not related exclusively to security level, but to a combination of factors. "A" class prisoners are rated highly on social status, education, style of living, character, and antecedents. They are eligible to spend their sentence in the open-air prison. Those who score low on the class criteria and/or who are convicted of offenses involving gross depravity of character or for offenses against society are not eligible for "A" class. They are considered the "B" class prisoners and serve their time in the closed prison.[3] Thus, inmates of foreign origin or of high caste and social status are routinely imprisoned under better conditions and segregated from inmates who are poorer and of lower social status. Larger and less crowded cells, access to books and newspapers and more and better food are available to the status "A" prisoners.

The major offenses for which the prisoners are interred are shown in table 18.1.

Prison Conditions

India's prisons are overcrowded. For example, Bombay Central Prison was built to accommodate 1,074 but in 2005 the average number of inmates was

TABLE 18.1.
India: Major Offenses for
Which Prisoners Are Interred

Offense Type	2005
Murder	53,086
Attempt to murder	7,787
Rape	5,392
Kidnapping and abduction	2,220
Robbery	18,730

Source: Indian Prison System

generally over 2,000. Around 180 prisoners live in a cell designed to house 50. Many sleep on blankets infested with lice. They also sleep in awkward positions making them susceptible to sexual overtures. Sodomy is rampant and there is a high prevalence of HIV and tuberculosis.

Jail wardens read all prisoner mail, coming in and going out.

There are activities available for inmates in most of India's prisons and they include sports, adult education, computer education, and vocational training. Every central prison has an elementary school with qualified teachers. Adult education is available for all inmates but attendance is optional. Prisoners can also enroll in distance education programs, such as university correspondence courses. Many inmates receive undergraduate and graduate degrees. Prisoners are often taught trades such as carpentry, tailoring, weaving, and bookbinding.

Women's Issues

A female inmate can keep her child until the age of five. As of 2005, there were about 1,392 children living in India's prisons. There are no separate facilities for the children. They share their mothers' bed, food, and utensils. Most prisons do not have crèches, medical care, or recreational and educational programs.

About 34 percent of the women prisoners were in the age group of 18 to 30, 49 percent 30 to 50, and 1 percent below 18. Among the convicted women, 66 percent were involved in offenses against another person. The educational standard of women prisoners is very low, with a 75 percent rate of illiteracy.

Women prisoners sentenced up to one month are confined in sub-jails, district prisons, and central prisons in separate enclosures or separate wards. However, long-term convicts and remand prisoners belonging to the cities of Hyderabad and Rajamundry are confined in two special prisons for women, located in Hyderabad and Rajamundry.[4]

Prison Staff

The custodial staff are ranked as follows: superintendent, jailer, deputy jailer, assistant jailer, head warders, and warders. Prison guards are known as warders. Warders must have a high school diploma and enroll in a six-month training program in disciplining, the principles of prison administration, and the practice of correctional procedure.

Parole

Parole is allowed in the form of emergency leave (15 days yearly) and ordinary leave (30 days annually) for participating in family events.

Visitation

Inmates must apply to have a person they wish to have visit. Such persons then fill out an application and prison officials perform a background check on the proposed visitor. If he or she is approved his or her name is placed on the inmates visiting list. The inmate then informs the prospective visitor when he may come. Minor children are only allowed to visit inmates when accompanied by their parent or legal guardian.

Notes

1. CIA, "India," *The World Factbook,* https://www.cia.gov/library/publications/the-world-factbook/geos/in.html (accessed October 20, 2007).
2. R. K. Raghavan, *World Factbook of Criminal Justice Systems, India* (1992), http://www.ojp.usdoj.gov/bjs/pub/ascii/wfbcjind.txt (accessed November 17, 2004).
3. International Centre for Prison Studies, "Prison Brief for India," *World Brief* (2006), http://www.kcl.ac.uk/depsta/rel/icps/worldbrief/continental_asia_records.php?code=94 (accessed February 3, 2006).
4. Penal Reform International, *Mental Health and Care of Women and Children in Prison in Andhra Pradesh (India)* (2005), http://www.penalreform.org/english/vuln_andhra.htm.

19

China

CHINA IS A UNITARY STATE ruled by a central government. Made up of 23 provinces, 5 autonomous regions, and 4 municipalities (Beijing, Chongqing, Shanghai, and Tianjin), China's population tops all countries with 1.3 billion inhabitants. China is in East Asia, bordered by the East China Sea, Korea Bay, Yellow Sea, and South China Sea, between North Korea and Vietnam.

The dominant ethnicity is Han Chinese at 91.9 percent. The remaining 8.1 percent are Zhuang, Uygur, Hui, Yi, Tibetan, Miao, Manchu, Mongol, Buyi, Korean, and other nationalities. The major religions are Daoism (Taoism) and Buddhism. Islam is represented by 1 percent to 2 percent and Christianity by 3 percent to 4 percent (2002 est.). The official languages are standard Chinese or Mandarin (Putonghua, based on the Beijing dialect), Yue (Cantonese), Wu (Shanghainese), Minbei (Fuzhou), Minnan (Hokkien-Taiwanese), Ziang, Gan, and Hakka dialects.[1]

China's highest state power is the People's National Control (NPC). The current constitution was adopted in 1982, and amended as recently as 1993.[2]

As of 2004, China's prison population was 1,548,498 at a rate of 118 per 100,000 population. Of those, 71,231 or 4.6 percent were female inmates.

There are 679 penal institutions in China. Only one of these prisons is under control of the Ministry of Justice. The remaining are under the control of provincial or municipal governments. Because of the prison system's decentralization, there is not one method for classifying the security levels of inmates and/or institutions. However, it is common for a range of five types of institutions to be present in a region.[3] The first are standard penitentiaries. The second type of penal institution is the reform-through-labor institutions.

Offenders at these institutions have been sentenced to serve at least a year in prison. There are also reform houses for juvenile delinquents. Juyi detention centers house offenders sentenced to less severe sentences, and Kanshou detention center houses offenders awaiting trial.[4]

The major offenses for which prisoners are interred are white collar crimes.

Women's Issues

As of 2004 there were 31 women's prisons in China. Of the 71,231 female inmates, 29,000 were charged with drug trafficking, robbery, murder, and prostitution.

On weekends the inmates are organized to take care of elderly people at local nursing homes. Psychologists from local universities are invited to give lectures to the inmates to solve some of their psychological problems. Lectures on women's health and psychology are given regularly. Women prisoners can be released on parole while pregnant and/or nursing. Women's prisons in China are all staffed with gynecologists to provide medical care.[5]

The women inmates are required to gain some legal knowledge as soon as they become inmates. They spend their first two months studying criminal law, criminal procedure, prison law, and the *Manual for Persons Serving Prison Terms* in order to acquaint them with their rights and obligations.

All the inmates who are able to work must do so. About 10 percent of the female inmates are unable to work following a doctor's examination or are too old to do so. Prisoners enjoy the same benefits as employees of state enterprises in terms of work hours, holidays, supply of food and occupational safety and health care.

China's treatment of its political prisoners, most recently members of the Falun Gong, is drastically different. Falun Gong members are beaten and tortured. For example, in one of the women's sections of the Masanjia Labor Camp, guards forced inmates to work at their sewing machines for 31.5 hours nonstop. During this time the guards kept threatening, cursing, and beating them. In other detention centers, there are reports that guards handcuff the women to the window bars, exhorting or demanding criminal inmates to beat them. The inmates are also forced to do all kinds of hard labor.

Prison Staff

The total institutional staff in China's prisons is 274,470 and the staff to prisoner ratio is 1:5.6. In November 2000, prison guards were given the first national proficiency and general knowledge exam. The tests were aimed at promoting the quality of prison police and facilitating the need for reforming and educating inmates. Officials in the Prison Management Bureau of the Justice Ministry announced that those who failed the test must receive training until they pass a makeup test. Those who fail the makeup test would be dismissed from their positions. In 2005, 2006, and 2007 Chinese prison staff were involved in training programs to enhance human rights protection of the inmates.

Parole

Chinese law contains provisions for stipulating a system for reducing sentences and release or parole. All prisoners who qualify and show true repentance or outstanding behavior may be granted a reduction in their sentence or released on parole. In 1990, 16 percent of prisoners had their sentences commuted or were released on parole. In 1991, the figure was 18 percent. Release on parole for medical treatment is also granted to all seriously ill inmates.

Visitation

The right of prisoners to family visits is provided for in both domestic law and in relevant international standards. Chinese prisoners can only be visited by family members and at most twice per month. A recent survey found that about 50 percent of Chinese prisoners were granted visits at least once a month. The visitors, who are usually family members, are expected to bring the inmate bedding, towels, toothpaste, soap, sanitary napkins, and other goods.

Notes

1. CIA, "China," *The World Factbook*, https://www.cia.gov/library/publications/the-world-factbook/geos/ch.html (accessed October 20, 2007).

2. Gary Bennett, ed., "China Facts and Figures," *Annual Handbook* 20 (Gulf Breeze, FL: Academic International Press, 1996).

3. Jianan Guo, Guo Xiang, Wu Zongxian, Xu Zhangrun, Peng Xiaohui, and Li Shuangshuang, *World Factbook of Criminal Justice Systems, China* (1992), http://www.ojp.usdoj.gov/bjs/pub/ascii/wfbcjchi.txt (accessed November 15, 2004).

4. Ibid.

5. "Chinese Prisons Get Woman's Touch," *People's Daily* (2002), http://english.people.com.cn/200208/24/eng20020824_101995.shtml (accessed February 21, 2006).

20

Japan

JAPAN IS LOCATED IN EASTERN ASIA. It is an island chain between the North
Pacific Ocean and the Sea of Japan. Japan has a population of 127,433,494
(July 2007 est.). The majority ethnicity is Japanese at 98.5 percent. The
remaining 1.5 percent is made up of Koreans (0.5 percent), Chinese (0.4
percent), and other (0.6 percent) (2004). The religions mostly observed are
Shinto and Buddhism, at 84 percent. Other religions make up the remaining
16 percent. The official language is Japanese.[1]

Japan has a federal system of government, but one that is largely centralized. The government is divided into executive, legislative, and judicial
branches and much of their political system was influenced by nineteenth-
century German and British parliamentary models.

Historically, Japan's legal system has been influenced by German criminal
law and French civil law. But in the era after World War II, American law
models became dominant. Japan has an informal system based on mediation.
Arbitration is also very popular.

With the onset of the Meiji Era (1867–1912), Western culture was introduced and the government established new laws reflecting a gradually
modernizing Japanese society. Criminal laws and prison laws were passed
that hastened modernization. Japan adopted the adversarial system with their
new constitution in 1996. Japan's criminal code is found in the 1948 Code
of Criminal Procedure and the 1949 Rules of Criminal Procedure under the
Constitutional Law. Japan's laws reflect American legal concepts in contexts
important to the protection of human rights.

TABLE 20.1.
Japan: Convicts in Prisons and
Detention Houses by Type of
Offense, 2002.

Offense Type	2002
Arson	310
Breaking and entering	565
Forgery	252
Rape	837
Gambling	29
Homicide	600
Assault	2,962
Larceny/theft	8,213
Robbery	1,371
Fraud	2,169
Extortion	882

Source: Judicial System and Research Department, 2002.

As of 2005, there were 76,413 prisoners in Japan for a rate of 60 per 100,000 population. Of those 4,508 or 5.9 percent were female prisoners.

The major offenses for which the prisoners were interred are shown in table 20.1.

There are 189 penal institutions with an occupancy level of 105.9 percent. The total institutional staff is 16,469 and the staff to prisoner ratio is 1:4.5.

Prison Conditions

Prison rules and regulations are strictly enforced and even the most trivial of offenses are dealt with in a swift and serious manner. Body searches and shake-downs of cells and property are common. All violations are documented by prison staff and result in a myriad of punishments:

- verbal reprimand
- suspension of remuneration
- prohibition of reading books or seeing pictures of family members
- suspension from work and/or exercise
- suspension of using self-furnished clothing and/or bedding
- reduction of food rations/choices
- solitary confinement

TABLE 20.2.
Japan: Programming Assignments for Inmates

Class E	Need for schooling
Class G	Need for guidance in daily life (primarily juveniles)
Class O	Suitable for open treatment
Class N	Suitable for accounting work
Class S	Need for special protection and care
Class T	Need for therapeutic treatment
Class V	Need for vocational training

Source: A. Didrick Castberg, *Japanese Criminal Justice* (New York: Praeger Publishers, 1990).

Programming in Japanese prisons exists in seven different areas. Inmates are assigned to these areas (called "classes") based on a determination from the Ministry of Justice, as shown in table 20.2.[2]

Women's Issues

Mothers are allowed to keep their babies with them for up to one year. Work opportunities for women inmates include the usual domestic type work, that is, tailoring, knitting, weaving, but in addition women are offered the opportunity to have training in fork lift driving and boiler operation. They may also receive training to obtain a license for care service for the elderly which is a very popular choice and very useful for the women inmates in obtaining employment after they are released.

Prison Staff

Notable differences can be seen between Japan and Western countries in the roles undertaken by prison staff, namely correctional officers. Over a century ago, the Japanese government included correctional services in the life-employment system, granting extensive training and instilling occupational values well beyond income.[3] Correctional officers are systematically recruited and attend a school specifically designed to train them in areas such as: penal procedures, penology, prison construction, budgetary accounting, and the treatment of juveniles. Once placed on the job, officers are expected to carry out three specific roles: security monitor, moral educator, and lay counselor. This is strikingly different to Western systems in that officers are expected to play the role of "an older brother or father figure" instead of keeping a social distance in order to avoid manipulation from inmates.[4]

Parole

As of 2002, the number of inmates imprisoned for life who were granted parole declined sharply. Of the 1,047 prisoners sentenced to life imprisonment, only six were granted parole. Around 30 were granted parole 10 years ago.

In 1995, the average jail time prior to parole exceeded 20 years. Prisoners who were released in 1989 served an average of 18 years, 10 months prior to parole and between 1977 and 1988 they served an average of between 15 years, 5 months and 16 years, 8 months in prison. The Ministry of Justice reported that it was reluctant to parole prisoners serving indefinite jail terms because of opposition from crime victims or their relatives.

Visitation

Visitors are allowed for all prisoners above 14 years of age. Visitors are usually relatives, but others may be allowed if the circumstance demands it. Visits are permitted only during the business hours of the prison. Except in the case the visitor is a lawyer, the interview may not last more than 30 minutes.

The more serious the offense the less frequent the visits. Thus for criminals sentenced to detention visits are allowed once a day. Visits for those under sentence of imprisonment are allowed once a month and for those sentenced to penal servitude once in two months. All visits must be held in the reception room unless the prisoner is ill. The visit must be in the presence of a prison officer and no foreign language may be used except by the permission of the governor.

Notes

1. CIA, "Japan," *The World Factbook*, https://www.cia.gov/library/publications/the-world-factbook/geos/ja.html (accessed October 20, 2007).

2. A. Didrick Castberg, *Japanese Criminal Justice* (New York: Praeger Publishers, 1990).

3. Elmer H. Johnson, "Opposing Outcomes of the Industrial Prison: Japan and the United States Compared," *International Criminal Justice Review* 4, no. 1 (1994): 52–57.

4. Ibid.

VIII
OCEANIA

21

Australia

A USTRALIA IS LOCATED IN OCEANIA. It is a continent between the Indian Ocean and the South Pacific Ocean. Australia has a population of 21,007,310 (July 2008 est.); 92 percent of the population is Caucasian, 7 percent are Asian, the remaining 1 percent are Aboriginal and other ethnicities. The majority of people are Christian (Roman Catholic, 26.4 percent; Anglican, 20.5 percent; other Christian, 20.5 percent). Other religions make up the remaining 32.6 percent of the population. English is spoken by 79.1 percent of the population, Chinese by 2.1 percent, and other/unspecified by 18.8 percent.[1]

Similar in many ways to the United States, Australia is a federalist (commonwealth) government composed of a national government and six state governments.[2] The commonwealth is responsible for the enforcement of its own laws. Notably, the most frequently prosecuted offenses in the commonwealth are those related to the importation of drugs and the violation of social security laws. The development of criminal law lies with the states. Local governments can pass legislation for the more minor social nuisance offenses. These laws, known as bylaws, carry a maximum penalty of a monetary fine. However, nonpayment of fines can result in imprisonment.[3]

The Australian legal system, derived from that of the United Kingdom, uses the parliament to make laws. The legal system is adversarial in nature and places a high value on the presumption of innocence. There are nine separate legal systems in operation, one for each state, the federal government, the Australian Capital Territory and the Northern Territory. Although there are some significant differences among these systems, they are essentially similar in nature.

As of 2004, there were 24,171 prisoners in Australia for a rate of 120 per 100,000 population. Of those, 1,668 or 6.9 percent were female prisoners.

There are 124 penal institutions with an occupancy level of 105.9 percent. Overall, Australian prisons suffer from overcrowding. Most recent data show that the official capacity for all prisons is 20,503 inmates. When this capacity is compared to the actual prison population total, Australian prisons, on average, are operating at over 117 percent capacity.

The total institutional staff for prisons is 8,059 and the staff to prisoner ratio is 1:2.5.

Table 21.1 describes offenses for which prisoners are incarcerated by gender.

Prison Conditions

Australian prisons are plagued by high levels of internal violence, riots, and insufficient staffing levels. In the Supermax prison in New South Wales prisoners are kept in cells that measure 2 by 3 meters for 22 hours or more a day. When an inmate enters the prison he or she is kept in segregation for two weeks. In 2007, the Human Rights and Equal Opportunity Commission (HREOC) reported that conditions in which mentally ill inmates are kept violates the prohibition on cruel, inhuman, or degrading treatment or pun-

TABLE 21.1.
Australia: Prisoners by Offense Type and Gender, 2003

Offense	Female	Male
Assault	126	2,039
Drug offense	166	1,674
Fraud	109	442
GSJ*	115	1,277
Homicide	122	1,767
Other theft	123	1,135
Other**	101	2,111
Robbery	134	2,401
Sex offense	9	2,007
Unlawful entry	115	2,105
Total	1,120	16,958

Source: Australian Bureau of Statistics, 2003
*Government security and justice procedures, includes offenses such as: breach of court order, breach of parole, escape custody, offenses against justice procedures, treason, sedition, and resisting customs officials.
**Includes other offenses against person and property, public order offenses, and driving offenses.

ishment.[4] In its 2007–2008 report HREOC reported that many women with mental illness were inappropriately detained in prison while their mental health needs were left unattended.[5] The report also stated that Indigenous women were especially at risk of discrimination in prison.

Women's Issues

Half of all the female inmates in prison have been imprisoned before. In 1999, 31 percent of all women were incarcerated for violent offenses (compared to 46 percent of men). Women are more likely than men to be incarcerated for drug offenses (12 percent compared to 9 percent for men) and property offenses (34 percent compared to 23 percent for men). The overwhelming majority of women (around 80 percent) were unemployed or not part of the labor force when entering prison and only 20 percent have completed secondary school.[6]

Recent research has estimated that there are 38,500 children in Australia who experience the incarceration of a parent per year. Of greater significance, it is estimated that 145,000 children currently under the age of 16 have lived through such an event, of whom approximately 24,000 have experienced maternal incarceration.[7] This represents just under 5 percent of all children living in Australia.

Prison Staff

During the late 1970s and early 1980s, prison reform caused a shift in hiring practices whereby females were hired as correctional officers in male occupied prisons. In South Australia, women were hired for correctional officer duties in 1983, and by 1986 comprised 9 percent of the custodial staff.[8] Not only were custodial duties now open to both men and women, but other positions, such as social workers and welfare officers, were also offered equally to both sexes.[9]

Parole

All prisoners other than those serving life sentences (or fixed terms of imprisonment) are entitled to be released from prison after they have completed their minimum term of imprisonment which the court set when they were sentenced. Whether inmates are released on parole depends upon their behavior in prison and their responses to rehabilitation programs. The decisions concerning their release and the revocation of their parole and return to prison are made by the

Parole Board. The Court of Criminal Appeal has the power to review Parole Board decisions.

A person who commits an offense while on parole risks being sent back to prison to serve the balance of the original sentence (that is, the balance of that sentence remaining as of the day the new offense was committed).

Incarceration of Indigenous People

There is widespread acknowledgement of the overrepresentation of Indigenous people (Aboriginal and Torres Strait Island descent) in Australian prisons. Most data show that Indigenous adults represent less than 2 percent of the Australian adult population but comprise approximately 19 percent of the total Australian prison population.[10] In fact, imprisonment rates show that incarceration of Indigenous people has been steadily increasing each year since the late 1980s.[11] Regional data show an even higher rate occurring in police lock-ups. These data provide a clear example as to why Australian Aborigines are frequently referred to as the most imprisoned race in the world. While research into the causes of this nationwide overrepresentation remains sparse, there is a general agreement that structural issues such as poverty, racism, and the destruction of culture are key elements of this overrepresentation.[12]

Visitation

Detainees are permitted a maximum of one noncontact visit per week with family members for up to one hour. This visit takes place in a visit box, with the detainees separated from the visitors by thick glass.

In the case of detainees with children under the age of 16, the detainees are permitted one contact visit per month for a maximum of one hour. The detainees are strip searched both before and after each of these visits. This visit occurs in a room measuring approximately 2 meters by 2.5 meters. Throughout the visit, the detainees remain in leg irons and in manacles attached to a leather band around the waist. Spouses and partners are not permitted in the room with the children but are instead required to observe the visit from behind thick glass.

Private Prisons

Australia currently has seven privately run prisons: two in Queensland and Victoria, and one each in Western Australia, New South Wales, and Southern

Australia. Each prison, along with their pertinent characteristics and contracted management, is described below.

Borallon Correctional Center, Queensland

Borallon was opened in January 1990, through contracts with Management & Training Corporation and the Queensland Corrective Services Commission. It is a medium- and maximum-security prison for males, with a capacity of 492 inmates.[13] Borallon offers several different types of programming including: anger management, substance abuse prevention—Alcoholics Anonymous, Narcotics Anonymous, Cocaine Anonymous—as well as vocational training (information technology, engineering, construction, and literacy).

Arthur Gorrie Correctional Center, Queensland

AGCC was opened in June 1992 through contracts with the Commission and the GEO Australia Group. It is a maximum-security reception and remand center for males, with a capacity of 710 inmates.[14] The center provides programming in substance abuse and anger management, as well as limited vocational programs in woodworking and textiles, with 20 inmates employed in each program.[15]

Port Phillip Prison, Victoria

PPP was opened in September 1997 through contracts with the Victoria Department of Justice and GSL Australia. It is a maximum-security prison for remanded and sentenced males, with a capacity for 710 inmates.[16] The prison is comprised of 13 separate units, each having a kitchen, tea-room, laundry area, day room, recreation area, and an outdoor courtyard. Inmates' cells are private, and each has a shower, wash basin, and toilet, as well as a desk, chair, television set, kettle, shelves, intercom, and bed.[17] PPP has a hospital ward with 20 beds.

Fulham Correctional Center, Victoria

Fulham was opened in March 1997 through contracts with the Victoria Department of Justice and the GEO Australia Group. It is a minimum/medium-security prison for males, with a capacity for 777 inmates.[18] Inmates in Fulham are typically considered mainstream offenders, and are housed according to security risk in either cell blocks (most restricted), lodges, or cottages (least restrictive).[19] Fulham offers a drug and alcohol treatment program as well as an inmate protection unit.

Acacia Prison, Western Australia

Acacia Prison was opened in 2001, through contracts with the Western Australia Department of Corrections and Australian Integrated Management Services. The prison is located approximately 50 km (31 mi) east of Perth. It is a medium-security prison for males, with a capacity of 750 inmates.[20] Acacia is an example of a campus-style prison where an inmate's freedom of movement is enhanced by the availability of open spaces. Acacia has also taken advantage of technologically advanced methods for managing inmates through the issuance of "smart cards." These cards store an inmate's identity as well as other necessary information, and are used to gain entry to certain areas of the prison, to access financial accounts, and to make purchases from the cafeteria and commissary.[21] Most inmates live in single cells which come equipped with a shower, basin, and toilet. Acacia also utilizes self-care units, where appropriately determined inmates are allowed to live removed from the general population, cook their own meals, and do their own laundry.[22]

Acacia has undergone one performance evaluation which determined that the prison has performed consistently with initial objectives. The report stated that there was a development of a positive culture with a focus on rehabilitation and reparation.[23] The most common recommendations were strategies for sharing information among public prisons.

Junee Prison, New South Wales

Junee Prison was opened in 1993 through contracts with New South Wales Department of Corrective Services and GEO Australia. Junee is the only private prison in New South Wales, and is located 450 km (280 mi) southwest of Sydney. Staff at Junee totals 207, with 125 full-time and casual custodial officers.[24] It is a minimum/medium-security prison for males, with a capacity for 600 inmates.[25]

Junee offers several types of programs to meet inmates' needs. Prison industries include: power cord assembly, electric kettle and jug assembly, and moccasin making. Available education courses consist of: commercial cooking, hospitality services, small business management, literacy, computer studies, aboriginal cultures, automobile studies, basic engineering, visual arts, fork lift operation, and rural studies. Special programs include: harm reduction and anger management, drug and alcohol discussion groups, and an HIV/AIDS program.[26]

Mount Gambier Prison, South Australia

Mount Gambier Prison was opened in April 1995 through contracts with the South Australia Department of Justice and GSL Australia. It is a minimum/medium-security prison for males, with a capacity for 110 inmates.[27] The prison is also able to accommodate short-term, high-risk male and female remandees. Mount Gambier incorporates a cottage and cell block design. Inmates are able to gain privileges through incentive-based contracts, and by participating in education and vocational training.[28]

Medium-security accommodation is provided in four two-story buildings housing up to 78 prisoners in each. Each building is divided into two blocks containing 39 cells. Medium-security lodges each house 17 prisoners. In each lodge there are 17 bedrooms, communal kitchen/dining room, lounge, and laundry.[29] Minimum-security accommodation for 100 prisoners is provided in cottage units. Each cottage has four single bedrooms, bathroom, laundry, lounge, kitchen and dining room. Prisoners in cottage accommodation prepare and cook their own meals and manage their own household budget.[30]

Notes

1. CIA, "Australia," *The World Factbook*, https://www.cia.gov/library/publications/the-world-factbook/geos/as.html (accessed November 4, 2008).

2. David Biles, *World Factbook of Criminal Justice Systems, Australia*, www.ojp.usdoj.gov/bjs/abstract/wfcj.htm (accessed October 13, 2008).

3. Ibid.

4. Human Rights and Equal Opportunity Commission, "Australia's Compliance with the Convention against Torture, and Cruel, Inhuman and Degrading Treatment" (February 2007), www.humanrights.gov.au.

5. Human Rights and Equal Opportunity Commission, *Annual Report 2007–2008*, www.humanrights.gov.au.

6. Australian Institute of Criminology, "Women in Prison—Numbers Soar" (October 31, 2000), http://www.aic.gov.au/media/2000.html.

7. S. Quilty, *The Health of the Children and Families of Prisoners* (Sydney: Sydney University, Faculty of Medicine, School of Public Health, 2003).

8. Adam Graycar and Peter Grabosky, eds., *The Cambridge Handbook of Australian Criminology* (Cambridge and New York: Cambridge University Press, 2002), 95.

9. P. Lynn and G. Armstrong, *From Pentonville to Pentridge: A History of Prisons in Victoria* (Melbourne: State Library of Victoria, 1996).

10. David Brown, "Mandatory Sentencing: A Criminological Perspective," *Australian Journal of Human Rights* 7, no. 2 (2001).

11. Aboriginal and Torres Strait Islander Commission, ATSIC (1997), 76.

12. Royal Commission into Aboriginal Deaths in Custody (1991).

13. Management & Training Corporation, http://www.mtctrains.com/corrections/facilties_borralon.php (accessed November 20, 2008).

14. The GEO Group, Inc., "What We Do," http://www.thegeogroupinc.com/whatwedo.asp (accessed November 20, 2008).

15. Ibid.

16. Victorian Prison System, VIC (2005).

17. Ibid.

18. Ibid.

19. Ibid.

20. Public Accounts Committee, "Value for Money from NSW Correctional Centres," Report No. 13/53 (No. 156) (September 2005).

21. Lenny Roth, "Privatisation of Prisons," Background Paper No. 3/04 (NSW Parliamentary Library Research Service, Australian Integrated Management Services, 2005), http://74.125.93.132/search?q=cache:vsir3kAnKigJ:www.parliament (accessed July 22, 2009).

22. Public Accounts Committee, "Value for Money."

23. Ibid.

24. Lenny Roth, *Privatisation of Prisons,* Background Paper No. 03-04, NSW Parliamentary Library Research Service (2005).

25. Ibid.

26. Ibid.

27. *Annual Report 2003–2004,* http://www.corrections.sa.gov.au/annual_report/2003-2004/custodial_ 2005 (accessed November 20, 2008).

28. Ibid.

29. Ibid.

30. Ibid.

Concluding Remarks

O F ALL THE COUNTRIES INCLUDED IN THIS STUDY, the United States has the highest number of prisoners per total population. Russia has the second highest number. India and Nigeria have the lowest number. Even though India has the lowest number of prisoners per total population, it has the second highest number of prisons; the United States has the greatest number. But at over 300,000 prisoners India ranks fifth among the countries included in this study.

As shown in table B.2, the prisons in Iran and Brazil are the most crowded. At 8.7 percent the United States has the greatest number and highest percentage of female prisoners. At 1.9 percent Nigeria has the lowest percentage of female prisoners followed by South Africa at 2.2 percent and Israel at 2.3 percent.

The offenses for which inmates are most often incarcerated are robbery and drugs.

The United States was the first country to open private prisons and it is the largest operator of private prisons. As of 2000, there are private prisons in Canada, the United Kingdom, Germany, Australia, Israel, and South Africa.

Comparing prison conditions in the 21 countries, we found, not unexpectedly, that the less developed countries had more crowded prisons and ones in which conditions were deplorable. France may be an exception to that observation. In 2005, the International Observatory of Prisons reported that the cells in French prisons were overcrowded, filthy, and rat infested. It also reported that France had the highest suicide rate among prisoners in Europe. In Nigeria, inmates sleep on concrete floors. Toilets are little more than holes in the floor and are usually overflowing. Lack of food is a major problem. In Egypt, many of the cells have no toilets, running water, or mattresses. Prisoners are often victims of torture by prison guards. In Brazil, violence among inmates is a frequent problem due in large part to a corrupt staff who allow weapons and drugs into the facilities, and the organization of gangs within the prisons.

In the Russian Federation inadequate food and medical supplies account for a high prevalence of starvation and death. As of 2006, more than 50,000 inmates had tuberculosis, 35,000 were HIV positive and nearly 90,000 were drug addicts.

In all of the countries women inmates are housed in separate facilities from male inmates. The United States is unusual among the developed countries in not allowing women to keep their babies in the early months or years of infancy. In many countries women may keep the babies for up to three years.

The prison guards in Brazil are noted for their use of beatings and killings of the inmates. As stated in the chapter on Brazil, in October 2006, 14 prison officials were convicted of torturing 35 inmates at a juvenile detention center in São Paulo. In Italy, prison directors must be university graduates with a law degree. The prison guards are members of the police force.

In Sweden, 43 percent of all prison staff are women and over 70 percent of the probation officers are women. Like Brazil, security officers in Egypt are reported by Amnesty International to ill-treat and sexually abuse inmates. In Japan, correctional officers must attend a school specifically designed to train them in penal procedures, penology, prison construction, budgetary accounting, and the treatment of juveniles. Officers are expected to carry out three specific roles: security monitor, moral educator, and lay counselor. They are expected to play the role of an older brother or father figure.

All of the countries have a system whereby prisoners are eligible for parole after serving some portion of their sentence. In June 2008, a bill was introduced into the national legislature in Nigeria that would grant parole to prisoners on grounds of good behavior.

Under widely varying conditions, all of the countries allow visitations for prison inmates. The relationship of the visitor to the inmate, the frequency of visits, the length of time per visit, and the conditions under which the visits take place are among the variations. Once a week is the most frequent time per visit and the longest time per visit is a whole day (for those who come from long distances). In Hungary in addition to receiving visitors once a month, as a reward for good behavior an inmate may be allowed to leave the prison for a weekend or other shorter periods of time. Visitations are most difficult in Nigeria because prisoners are frequently transferred to prisons that are farthest from their homes. In Egypt, as of September 2004, some prisoners are permitted to leave the prison for 48 hours and visit with their families.

With these remarks we conclude our account of prisons the world over.

Appendix A

Political Prisoners

I N THIS APPENDIX, WE REPORT the number and types of political prisoners among the countries included in this study. We adopt the definition of political prisoner from that used by Amnesty International, that is, persons held in prison or otherwise detained for their involvement in political activity and/or for their religious or philosophical beliefs. They are also persons who are deemed by a government to either challenge or threaten the authority of the state.

The countries included in appendix A are China, Egypt, Iran, Israel, the Russian Federation, and a brief comment about the United States.

China

Among the recent major group of political prisoners in China are members of a religious group known as the Falun Gong, a spiritual practice that was founded in China by Li Hongzhi in 1992. The Falun Gong's teachings deal with such issues as the "cultivation of virtue and character," "moral standards for different levels," and "salvation of all sentient beings." Falun Gong draws on oriental mysticism and traditional Chinese medicine. It borrows the language of modern science to represent its cosmic laws. Rather then being a religious faith, Falun Gong practitioners see it as a new form of science.

Falun Gong does not have a roster of its members, but in 1998 the Chinese government published a figure of 70 million practitioners in China. Clearwidsom.net, a Falun Gong website, claims 100 million practitioners in more than 80 countries.

What follows has been taken in total from the Falun Gong website, Clear-wisdom.net. It provides a detailed picture of the treatment Falun Gong prac-titioners claim they receive in Chinese prisons.

Criminal Prisoners Incited to Brutally Torture Ms. Liu Dan in Heilongjiang Province Women's Forced Labor Camp

(Clearwisdom.net) Falun Dafa practitioner Ms. Liu Dan is 29 years old and from Jixi City in Heilongjiang Province. She was arrested and sent to Heilongji-ang Province Women's Forced Labor Camp on March 1, 2006. At one time she went on a hunger strike for several months. On October 3, 2006, criminal inmate monitor Han Ying beat her brutally, so she went on a third hunger strike. She has resisted the persecution and suffered brutal torture at the hands of criminal inmates. It is now March 2, and Ms. Liu is now extremely thin and weak.

Practitioner Ms. Li Yushu from Mohe City in Heilongjiang Province was il-legally placed in the same women's forced labor camp. She has been on a hunger strike for two years and seven months. Her persecution continues and all infor-mation about her situation at the labor camp is being strictly blocked. Details are very limited.

Head inmate monitor Zhao Li led monitors Zhang Fangqing, Zhou Fengli, Xiu Shufen, and others in brutally torturing Ms. Liu Dan from November 29, 2006, to December 9, 2006. Ms. Liu was put in prison hospital room 302. There is no video monitoring equipment in the room. Zhao Li and Zhou Fengli forced Ms. Liu to wear prisoner clothes with words that slander Falun Dafa. They pulled her off the bed and onto the floor. Ms. Liu was extremely weak at the time, but she did not cooperate. She yelled, "Falun Dafa is good," until Zhao Li and Zhou Fengli taped her mouth shut. Then they pulled an arm over her shoulder, while twisting the other down and back until the hands could be tied together. They left her like this for long periods of time. At other times, they tied Ms. Liu's hands together using shirts and towels. They continuously cursed at her. Such torture was deadly for the weakened Ms. Liu. She had a heart attack, passed out, and was incontinent. She regained consciousness, vomiting uncontrollably. Criminal pris-oner Zhang Lirong was fearful of being held responsible for Ms. Liu's off-and-on unconsciousness. Zhang Lirong wanted to find a nurse, but Xiu Shufen would not let her. They argued for a long time and finally carried Ms. Liu to the bed. They hid the signs of vomiting. Nurse Luo Yumei found Ms. Liu's blood pressure to be extremely low when she came to check on her. She asked Ms. Liu how long she had been like that, but Zhao Li quickly said it was only a short time. Immediately afterwards, Zhao Yingling (the head of the forced labor camp), Zhang Xiuli (an instructor), and Yu Yingmin (a brigade captain) all came into the room. They screamed, "Who told her that she could lie on the bed? Get down on the floor and sit still! Sit still until 10 p.m.!" Zhao Li pulled Ms. Liu off the bed and onto the floor. Ms. Liu was still only half-conscious.

With Head Zhao Yingling's knowledge and approval, Zhao Li and other criminal inmates tortured Ms. Liu even more brutally. Almost every day, they forced Ms. Liu to sit still on the ground for hours. One day, Ms. Liu was forced to sit still on the floor for 24 hours, with both hands tied to the bed and her mouth taped shut.

The morning of December 2, 2006, Director Liu Zhiqiang and Brigade Captain Zheng Jie were in room 303. Ms. Liu, in room 302 across the hall, heard them and yelled out, "Persecution!" Zhang Fangqing, Zhao Li and Zhou Fengli got really nervous. Once again they started the inhumane tortures. They tied Ms. Liu's arms behind her back and to the side of the bed. That position would not allow Ms. Liu to squat down or stand up. Zhang Fangqing pulled hair out of Ms. Liu's head, twisted it together, and stuck it into Ms. Liu's nose and ears. They took turns violently cursing at Ms. Liu for almost an entire day. They did not put Ms. Liu back in the bed until the nurse came to force-feed her.

Inmate Zhang Fangqing taught Zhao Li how to torture people. Every day after that, inmate Zhao Li pulled Ms. Liu to the ground to brutally beat and kick her for a while. Then she hung Ms. Liu up by her hair. Soon her hair was all over the floor. She slapped Ms. Liu's face, stepped on her bare feet, and violently twisted Ms. Liu's hands behind her back repeatedly. If Ms. Liu vomited, Zhao Li would use paper to smear it all over Ms. Liu's face, neck, and ears. She would stick the paper to Ms. Liu's chest, rub Ms. Liu's socks in the vomit, and force them into Ms. Liu's mouth.

Ms. Liu told Sui Lijuan, a night shift inmate monitor, to find Captain Yu Yingmin and tell him about the persecution. Zhao Li heard about it and stopped Sui Lijuan. Ms. Liu then told Wang Hongzhi, another prisoner monitoring on the night shift, but none would report it to the captain. Ms. Liu had no choice but to try to get the police to help her. It is their job to deal with the prisoners who violate the prison rules. However, when they saw Ms. Liu tied up with her mouth taped, sitting still on the floor, they acted as if they hadn't seen a thing. There was no reason for Zhao Li to fear any punishment, so she tortured Ms. Liu even more brutally. She blatantly told Ms. Liu that nobody could help her now and nobody cared about stopping the persecution. Prison director Liu said that "transforming" Falun Gong practitioners was to be the main goal of the prison next year.

Yu Yingmin was on call December 9, 2006. Ms. Liu told her about the torture and showed Yu Yingmin her swollen arms and hands and the scars from Zhao Li scratching her mouth. Zhao Li heard her and screamed loudly from the hallway, "If Captain Yu changes the monitor, then she must be standing on Falun Gong's

*side. I'll tell Director Liu to inform the brigade." Later, Zhao Li was transferred
and the persecution of Ms. Liu finally eased up.*

*The prisoners who torture practitioners are given special rights. While in jail
they can enter and leave the rooms at will, do whatever they want, and report
anyone to the police.*[1]

*We call for just and righteous forces in China and overseas to rescue Falun
Gong practitioners who are currently under persecution.*

Tibetan Political Prisoners

Another group of people who are currently targets of Chinese oppression
are Tibetans who are opposed to Chinese rule of their country. In 1999 there
were 1042 Tibetan political prisoners in Chinese prisons in Tibet.[2] Among the
more than twenty prisons located in Tibet there are political prisoners in each
of them. Drapchi Prison is one of the worst Chinese prisons and has the worst
record in Tibet for death due to severe abuse. At least 25 Tibetan inmates died
as a result of severe abuse between 1989 and 2008. Over 620 political prisoners
have been held in Drapchi since 1987. The conditions in the other prisons in
Tibet are described below.[3]

Drapchi Prison: Drapchi Prison, officially TAR Prison Number One, is
situated in the northeast outskirts of Lhasa City, a short bicycle ride
from several tourist hotels. Over 620 political prisoners have been held
at Drapchi since 1987, out of which around 140 are still being detained
there. Drapchi is one of the worst Chinese prisons and has the worst record in Tibet for death due to severe abuse while in custody, with at least
25 deaths due to severe abuse since 1989.

Powo Tramo: Officially TAR Prison Number Two, Powo Tramo lies 650
kilometers east of Lhasa in Pome County, in the Kongpo Prefecture.
Seven political prisoners are currently serving sentences there, and since
1987, at least 16 have been held there. Powo Tramo is notorious for its
harsh conditions caused by cold, damp weather and difficult forced labor
linked to the forestry industry.

Lhasa Prison (Utritru): Lhasa Prison, formerly known as Utritru Prison,
is about three kilometers northeast of the Jokhang Temple, and is part
of a group of prisons collectively known as Sangyib. Despite its central
location, only 30 political prisoners have been held at Lhasa Prison, and
none are currently there. After the May 1998 protests at Drapchi though,
several political prisoners were held in the solitary confinement cells at
Lhasa Prison, as all those at Drapchi were occupied. Most of the forced
labor involves making bricks and cutting stone blocks.

Maowun Prison: Maowun Prison is situated in Ngaba Tibetan and Qiang Autonomous Prefecture, in Sichuan Province. Several political prisoners have been sent to Maowun from neighboring Kardze Tibetan Autonomous Prefecture (TAP). During the 1990s, at least 15 Tibetan political prisoners have been held at Maowun Prison, out of which eight are still serving sentences there.

Rang-nga-khang: The Rang-nga-khang is actually a network of prisons located in Dardo and Dawu counties, Kardze TAP. Prisoners are sent to gold mines there, and are made to fulfill daily excavation quotas despite meager food and little sleep. According to Tsering Dorje, who was detained there in the early 1990s, prisoners are often beaten there, sometimes so badly that limbs were broken and eyes dislodged. Several Chinese prisoners, who had no relatives to supplement food, were driven to suicide, while other prisoners injured or mutilated themselves to avoid excavation work. It is not clear how many Tibetan political prisoners are currently serving sentences there.

Other Prisons Where Tibetans Are Held

There are at least ten *laogai* in or around Xining, Qinghai Prefecture. At these *laogai* a variety of products, such as steel products, leather and fur clothes, and hydroelectric equipment are produced.

This is an area with a high Tibetan population, but it is not clear how many Tibetans are being detained there. It seems that many Tibetans are being held at the Hydroelectric Equipment Factory (234 out of a total of about 900 prisoners), and it has been reported that some political prisoners have been held there.

Trisam Laojiao: Trisam Laojiao opened in 1992, and is situated 14 kilometers to the west of Lhasa City center. About 170 political prisoners have been detained at Trisam, but only five are currently serving sentences there. Prisoners are made to work in the vegetable gardens or on construction sites, where they have to cut stone blocks and carry heavy stone blocks and bricks as well as other general building work. Prisoners work over eight hours a day, and are given days off about once a fortnight. The work is very strenuous and it is not uncommon for prisoners to faint while they are working. Prisoners sometimes become so weak that they cannot walk properly and have to lean on the wall for support.

Four prisoners are known to have died as a result of abuse at Trisam, three of them soon after release and one while in custody. The youngest victim was Sherab Ngawang, who was only 12 years old when she was arrested for joining an independence demonstration in 1992. She was sentenced to three years imprisonment and then sent to Trisam, where she was constantly being beaten, sometimes with electric prods. She died on April 17, 1995, at the age of 15. Reports from her funeral indicate that her stomach and kidneys were badly damaged.

Chamdo Laojiao: Chamdo Laojiao opened in 1998, and is near Chamdo, the capital of the Chamdo Prefecture. Six political prisoners have been held there, but none are believed to be serving sentences there now.

Xinhua Laojiao: Xinhua Laojiao is situated in Mianyang municipality, 220 km north of Chengdu, in northern Sichuan. The work done at Xinhua is mainly construction work. In October 1999, several protests were held against the arrest of a respected Buddhist teacher, Sonam Phuntsog, in Kardze county town, in Kardze TAP. Following these demonstrations twelve Tibetans are known to have been arrested and sent to Xinhua Laojiao.

At Xinhua, two Tibetans died last year. They collapsed while being forced to work in the hot summer weather last year. They were not given water or medical treatment and died shortly afterwards. One of those who died has been identified as Tsering Wangdrak, who was married with two young children. He was reportedly beaten unconsciousness at least once while he was being detained at Kardze county PSB Detention Center, and continued to be beaten at Xinhua.

Gutsa PSB Detention Center: This is the Lhasa's prefectural PSB Detention Center, and is situated a few kilometers east of Lhasa City center. In the period since 1987, more political prisoners have been detained at Gutsa than anywhere else. Most of the political prisoners sentenced to Drapchi undergo interrogation at Gutsa, and many more are detained for a while and then released without charge.

Prison officers at Gutsa are renowned for the barbaric measures they use while interrogating prisoners: beatings are standard and electric prods are often used. According to Gyaltsen Choetso: "When I was first taken to Gutsa, they stripped me naked and used electric prods and beat me all over my body. There were around 60 or 70 prison guards who tortured prisoners and beat us with iron rods and wooden sticks." At least four people have died as a direct result of abuse at Gutsa.

Sitru PSB Detention Center: One of the Sangyib family of prisons, Sitru is situated to the north of Lhasa Prison. Many of those held at Sitru have been suspected of having had contact with "foreigners," especially Tibetans living in exile, or have been abroad themselves, and have been accused of trying to send human rights information out of the country. Over 110 political prisoners have been detained at Sitru.

Shigatse (Nyari) PSB Detention Center. Shigatse Prefecture PSB Detention Center, colloquially known as Nyari, is where Tibetans who are caught trying to cross the Tibet-Nepal border without proper documentation are generally held.

Public Security Bureau (PSB) Detention Centers

Many political prisoners have also been held at Lhoka and Chamdo Prefectures' PSB Detention Centers. It is not clear how many are currently being detained at either of these sites.

Falun Gong practitioners and Tibetans comprise the overwhelming majority of political prisoners in China today.

Egypt

As of 2008 there are about 17,000 political prisoners in Egypt, according to the Egyptian Organization of Human Rights; a majority of the prisoners are Islamists. The Muslim Brotherhood is one Islamist group.

According to an article in the *New York Times* (August 2008) the Egyptian Organization for Human Rights charges that torture and sexual abuse of prisoners has become so widespread that it "now appears to be a matter of policy by security forces holding persons detained for both political and nonpolitical reasons. According to the report security forces use whips, electric prods and electric shock treatment to sensitive parts of inmates' bodies as well as water hoses to extract confessions. Detainees are beaten immediately on arrival at the prison. The practice has become known as 'one of the rites greeting political prisoners on arrival in prisons.'"

In a report by Amnesty International, the authors claim that

the lack of adequate medical care and facilities, resulted in, or contributed to, the ill health of large numbers of prisoners, the rapid spread of diseases throughout prisons (the most commonly occurring problems include asthma, pulmonary pneumonia, and skin diseases), and the deaths in custody of at least four individuals in 1996. Furthermore, in some prisons, security officers routinely torture and ill-treat prisoners. Amnesty International is concerned that the practice of torture and ill treatment in prisons is facilitated by the administrative detention of thousands of individuals, and by the incommunicado detention of those held in the high-security prison in Tora and Istiqbal.

According to information received by Amnesty International, most Egyptian prisons lack even the most basic medical facilities necessary for the treatment of prisoners' health problems. Most prisons have no medical personnel on site, and only basic medication such as analgesics and cream for the treatment of skin diseases, such as scabies, are available. Both the High Security Prison in Tora and al-Fayoum Prison reportedly receive no more than one-weekly visits by doctors, who dispense only the most basic of medicines. Amnesty International has also received reports that seriously ill prisoners in need of specialized care have not been transferred to hospitals. The lack of adequate medical facilities and care in places of detention is in direct contravention of both international human rights standards and national legislation. The UN Body of Principles of the Protection of All Persons Under Any Form of Detention or Imprisonment (United Nations, 1988), principle 24, notes,

A proper medical examination shall be offered to a detained or imprisoned person as promptly as possible after his admission to a place of detention or imprisonment, and thereafter medical care and treatment shall be provided whenever necessary. This care and treatment shall be provided free of charge.[4]

The UN Principles of Medical Ethics relating to the care of prisoners and detainees, principle w, also state:

Health personnel, particularly physicians, charged with the medical care of prisoners and detainees have the duty to provide them with protection of their physical and mental health and treatment of disease of the same quality and standard as is afforded to those who are not imprisoned or detained.

Amnesty International has also received numerous reports providing information on serious overcrowding in Egyptian prisons. Large numbers of prisoners are housed in cramped and poorly ventilated cells in which the humidity often reaches unacceptably high levels, particularly during the summer. Prisoners are locked in their cells for the greater part of the day, and are often only allowed one hour per day in the fresh air. This confinement undoubtedly contributes to severe respiratory and allergy related ailments among prisoners, and to the rapid spread of contagious diseases such as scabies and other skin diseases. The outbreak and spread of disease is also exacerbated by the grossly inadequate standards of hygiene in Egyptian prisons. Water supplies and washing and toilet facilities are severely limited, and prisoners are not provided with sufficient clothing or blankets.

Inadequate diet is also a significant contributory factor in the ill health of prisoners. The Egyptian Law Regulating Prisons stipulates that prisoners' food rations should include 14 meals per week, to comprise seven bean dishes, three lentil dishes, two meat dishes, one cheese dish, one stewed vegetable dish, and a portion of dried dates. Each prisoner should also receive a bread and rice ration. Amnesty International has received reports that in practice this ration is never met, and that the food provided is usually virtually inedible—allegedly undercooked and contaminated with insects, and served in filthy buckets. Prisoners are often forced to rely on food provided by relatives or obtained on the black market inside the prison.

Torture and ill-treatment of political prisoners in Egyptian prisons have become widespread. In al-Wdi al-Gadid and al-Fayoum prisons for example, the torture and ill-treatment of prisoners begin upon their arrival, when they are subjected to a "Hafl al-Istiqbal" (welcome party) during which they are forced to crawl to their cells on their hands and knees between two lines of security officers who beat them until they arrive at their cells. Prisoners are thereafter reportedly subjected to routine beatings by security officers.

Amnesty International has issued many reports about the systematic use of torture against political prisoners in Egypt. It has submitted details of many cases to the Egyptian authorities, requesting that all allegations of torture be subjected to prompt, thorough, and impartial investigations and that the procedures followed and the findings of such investigations be made public within reasonable time. Though the Egyptian government has repeatedly stated to Amnesty International that all allegations of torture are investigated, the organization has received no responses to any of its requests for details of investigations carried out to date. In its May 1996 report, the UN Committee against Torture, too, concluded that "torture is systematically practiced by the Security forces in Egypt, in particular by State Security Intelligence."

Amnesty International fears that the torture and ill treatment of political prisoners in Egypt is facilitated by the practice of administrative detention (some detainees have been held for over six years without charge or trial) and by the prolonged incommunicado detention of large numbers of political prisoners. Political prisoners who are charged, and who claim to have been subjected to torture, may be examined by forensic medical doctors at the request of the public prosecutor's office, or the trial court. Administrative detainees, held without charge or trial, usually have no opportunity to submit a complaint about their treatment to the competent authorities. Prisoners held in the high-security prison in Tora and Istiqbal Tora Prison have had no access to lawyers or families since December 1993 and September 1994 (respectively, as a result of bans on visits to these prisons imposed by the Ministry of the Interior). Visits have also been banned for prolonged periods of time on several occasions to al-Fayoum Prison, opened in May 1995. These bans totally disregard both national legislation—articles 38, 39, and 40 of the Egyptian Law Regulating Prisons which guarantee prisoners' rights to visits by lawyers and families—and international human rights standards; Principle 15 of the Body of Principles states that "communication of the detained or imprisoned person with the outside world, and in particular his family or counsel, shall not be denied for more than a matter of days."

In September 2007, the Human Rights Organization issued a report in which they stated that "repression against independent human rights activists is increasing." The report goes on to state that "Two recent victims are Mohamed el-Derini and Ahmed Mohamed Sobh, who have been detained for speaking out to defend the rights of the small Shi'ite Muslim religious minority in Egypt, and for exposing and denouncing the use of torture in Egyptian prisons."

The two men are being held in solitary confinement at the Torah prison in Cairo. The State Security Prosecutor charged them with "disseminating Shi'ite extremist ideas with the intent of provoking contempt of the Islamic religion" and "spreading false rumors and sensational propaganda." The first charge appears to be linked to the two activists' Shi'ite Muslim faith and their activities to defend the rights of the small Shi'ite minority in Egypt. The charge of "spreading false rumors" is connected with their public denunciation of torture in Egyptian prisons.

The imprisonment of the two men coincides with a number of repressive measures taken in recent months by the government in what appears to be a growing clampdown on the independent Egyptian human rights community. In December 2006, the government shut down the Ahalina Center for Egyptian Family Support and Development that provides legal aid and health and social services to the deprived inhabitants of the city of Shubra Al-Khayma. In April 2007, the Egyptian authorities closed down the headquarters and two branches of the Center for Trade Union and Workers Services (CTUWS), an independent nongovernmental organization that provides legal aid to workers and monitors the situation of labor rights in Egypt. Last month, the government issued a decree dissolving the Association for Human Rights Legal Aid (AHRLA), an organization involved in exposing human rights violations and providing legal assistance to victims of torture.

On November 30, 2006, 12 men were convicted in Egyptian court for their role in a 2004 terrorist bombing in Taba. Thirty-four were killed in seaside resort attack. Two of the men were sentenced to death. All of the men claimed at trial that they had been tortured while in detention.

Muhammad Jayiz Sabah Hussein, one of the men sentenced to death, testified in court that he had been "blindfolded, bound, and unaware of his location," and that state security officers had "hung him by his arms and legs and used electrical currents to torture him" to extract confessions from him before his trial, according to Human Rights Watch. Doctors confirmed at trial that Jayiz had bodily marks consistent with his claim of torture.

The BBC has reported that "Egypt has been linked to extraordinary rendition, the practice of Western democracies of sending detainees to third-party countries for interrogation. Both the United States and the United Kingdom have sent terrorist suspects to Egypt for detention." In 2005, Egypt's prime minister acknowledged that since 2001 the United States had transferred some 60 to 70 detainees to Egypt as part of the "war on terror."

Iran

Political prisoners in Iran are housed together with regular criminal and juvenile offenders. Iranian officials, including the chief of the Prisons and Corrections Organization, claim there are no political prisoners in Iranian prisons. One explanation given by the prison chief is that parliament has not passed legislation defining political crimes.

But in 2005 known dissidents such as journalist Akbar Ganji, attorney Abdolfatteh Soltam, and student activist Ali Afshari were in prison for exposing the corruption and hypocrisies within the regime, defending dissidents, or participating in events that embarrassed the government.

Going back in time to 1988 the Iranian government executed thousands of political prisoners. Estimates range from 1,400 to 30,000. Most of them were members of a left-wing group called the People's Mojahedin Organization of Iran (PMOI). Among the specific charges against members of the PMOI were that they did not believe in Islam, they cooperated with Saddam Hussein in the war against Iran, they spread rumors against Iran, and they had connections with Western powers that were acting against Iran's independence. Most of the executed were either high school or college students or recent graduates, and about 10 percent were women.

Returning to the present time (2008), the Boston-based Women's Forum Against Fundamentalism in Iran (WFAF) reported:[5]

Tehran's fundamentalist regime has resorted to new strategies for killing political prisoners, particularly those who have gained an international attention and recognition. On September 6th, (2002) in a preemptive move, Tehran's regime announced that Mr. Valiollah Feyz Mahdavi has committed suicide in Ghohardasht prison. Mr. Mahdavi death followed the death of Mr. Akbar Mohammadi on July 30, 2006. Both political prisoners and had been on hunger strike protesting prison conditions and their detention on fabricated charges.

Mr. Feiz-Mahdavi, 28, and a member of Iran's main opposition group (PMOI/MeK), was arrested in 2001. He was sentenced to execution by the Tehran's regime, however, due to international pressure and a widespread campaign by human rights advocates in exile, his death sentence was put on hold in recent weeks. However, on September 3rd, his attorney, Mr. Mohammad Sharif, was told by the 6th District Prosecutor's Office of the Revolutionary Court in Tehran that his "client's execution sentence had not been commuted to imprisonment."

Mr. Mahdavi, who was on his seventh day of hunger strike, issued a statement from prison calling on the international community to continue their campaign on behalf of Iran's political prisoners. On the eighth day of his hunger strike, Mr. Mahdavi's health deteriorated tremendously, yet the prisoner's officials continued to ignore calls by other prisoners pleading medical attention for Mr. Mahdavi. Based on reports received from families of political prisoners in Iran, Mr. Mahdavi had a cardiac arrest before receiving any medical attention. He was revived in prison's medical facility, but was never returned to his cell. Many of his cellmates immediately issued statements and calls for investigation on Mr. Mahdavi's status.

In a move to avoid unwanted attention to the status of political prisoners, Tehran's regime announced his suicide on Wednesday September 6, 2006. Yet, based on reports received from underground human rights groups in Iran, the fundamentalist regime is now pressuring Mr. Mahdavi's cellmates to give on-camera testimony on his suicide. In the last two days, camera crews are interrogating prisoners in Gohardasht prison, where Mr. Mahdavi was murdered, to cover up the heinous act by Tehran's regime.

Women's Forum Against Fundamentalism in Iran (WFAFI) calls on the international community to pay attention to such evidence of blatant violations of rights and international norms. Tehran's regime must be strongly condemned by the international community. Ahmadinejad's regime must be held responsible for terror at home. His regime must also be referred to the United Nations Security Council for state-sponsor of violence against its own citizens. WFAFI calls upon the United Nations Human Rights Council, the United Nations Security Council, and the International Human Rights organizations to dispatch fact-finding missions to Iran and provide report on the status of political prisoners. The lives of political prisoners are in danger. The world must intervene to avoid another purge and massacre of political prisons in Iran.

Israel

With the exception of a very small number, political prisoners in Israel are practically all Palestinians. In March 2003 there were about 10,000 inmates in Israeli prisoners, 60 percent were imprisoned for criminal offenses, and 40 percent for terrorist and sabotage activities and for public safety offenses (such as placing incendiary devices in public places, throwing Molotov cocktails or rocks, assaulting civilians or security personnel). In 2004, the estimated number of political prisoners was 7,500 and among those there were about 100 Palestinian women.

As of 2005, family visits and telephone calls to security prisoners were banned. Thousands of Palestinian prisoners have been totally cut off from their families.

Some of the conditions that the prisoners are protesting include:[6]

- Subjecting prisoners to solitary confinement for excessive periods of time, for months and even years.
- Arbitrary imposition of financial penalties on prisoners for minor infractions, arbitrary revocation of visitation rights, and extended confinement to cells as punishment for minor infractions such as singing or speaking too loudly.
- Confining children with adult prisoners and political prisoners with criminals.
- Withholding or delaying medical treatment and the provision of medication to sick detainees.
- Severely restricting the category of family members entitled to visit prisoners thus denying visitation rights to other close family members.
- Arbitrary denial of travel permits to family members of prisoners living in the West Bank or Gaza so that they cannot travel to prisons to see their relatives.
- Imposing conditions on travel for family members and obstacles that result in travel of a few hours being prolonged to 16 or 17 hours for a 45-minute visit.
- Conducting humiliating strip searches of visiting family members even though they are usually separated from the prisoners by a full glass barrier as well as a wire mesh barrier.
- Providing such poor visitation facilities that prisoners find it difficult to see or hear their loved ones.
- Maintaining prisoners on near-starvation diets that are insufficient to sustain health.
- Applying rules concerning items that prisoners may receive from their families arbitrarily and inconsistently, on the whim of the guards, with each visit.
- Withdrawing studying privileges that in the past allowed prisoners to continue their high school or university studies through correspondence courses.

Of the 100 Palestinian women political prisoners about half are housed in Hasharon Prison. Human Rights has reported that the rooms are dirty and infected with mice and cockroaches. The heat is unbearable. The windows are closed and covered so that hardly any air or daylight can enter. The food is insufficient, of inferior quality or even spoilt. The women are prevented from receiving family visits.

A report published in October 2003 by Addameer Prisoners Support and Human Rights Association, entitled "Torture of Palestinian Political Prisoners in Israeli Prisons" states "Israel is the only country in the world to have legalized the use of torture, torture that in some cases has proven lethal."[7] Furthermore, Israel is amongst the few countries that have officially stated that it does not recognize the mandate of the Committee Against Torture to investigate claims of torture. Israel has continuously refused to cooperate with the committee in the collection of information and testimony concerning the practice of torture against Palestinian political prisoners by Israel since 1967. This is in spite of the fact that Israel ratified the Convention Against Torture.

Russian Federation

According to Amnesty International, the conditions in some prisons amount to cruel, inhuman, or degrading treatment.[8] Prisons are grossly overcrowded and thousands of prisoners have no individual bed and have to sleep in shifts, often without bedding. Many cells are filthy and pest-ridden, with inadequate light and ventilation. Food and medical supplies are frequently inadequate. The unsanitary conditions mean that illness spreads rapidly; lung, circulatory, and skin diseases, especially tuberculosis and scabies, are widespread. Mental illness is also common. In July 1995, 11 prisoners died of heatstroke in an overcrowded prison in Novokuznetsk, Kemerovo Region. Up to 25 people were being held in cells meant for 10 and the air temperature rose as high as 48 to 51°C.

Amnesty International has called on the Russian president to seek to ensure that the rights of vulnerable groups of people and specific professional groups, such as journalists, are protected and their safety ensured. There is a growing pattern of murders of journalists in the Russian Federation; in most of the cases the perpetrators have not been identified. In addition, there are a number of cases where persons are charged and detained on criminal charges, while the real motive for their persecution is allegedly political. One of the most recent cases to come to Amnesty International's attention concerns Viktor Orekhov, ex-KGB official and former dissident, who was sentenced to three years in a corrective labor colony on July 21, 1995. Viktor Orekhov was arrested in March 1995 following the discovery of a pistol during a search of his car by police, and was charged until Article 218 of the Criminal Code with possession of a firearm. Amnesty International was concerned that the criminal case against Viktor Orekhov was fabricated to punish him for making statements critical of a senior Russian security services official, and in retribution for past political activities in opposition to the KGB. He was released early from prison on March 21, 1996, in accordance with instructions issued by President Yeltsin on March 11, 1996.

Another similar case concerns Alexander Nikitin, a retired Russian naval officer who worked on a report on the dangers of nuclear waste in the Northern Fleet, for the Norwegian nongovernmental group Bellona Foundation, and was arrested on February 6, 1996, by the Federal Security Services (FSB) in St. Petersburg. He has been charged with treason under article 64 of the Russian Criminal Code which states that persons found guilty in these actions are sentenced to prison for 10 to 15 years, or to the death penalty. Alexander Nikitin's arrest took place in the context of an emerging pattern of persecution of environmental activists connected with the Bellona Foundation in Russia. Amnesty International urges the president to take a personal initiative in reviewing the circumstances of arrest and detention of people detained on the basis of their political activities; to order the release of anyone who is a prisoner of conscience (held solely for the nonviolent expression of political beliefs) and to ensure a fair and prompt trial for all political prisoners.

Journalist Grigory Pasko reports "The human rights congress that recently ended in Moscow adopted a resolution on political prisoners in Russia. Among other things, it says: 'In recent years in Russia, as in the USSR in its time, criminal cases are being fabricated, initiated by the special services on the orders of the political power of the country, spy-mania is being intensified. Officially recognized political prisoners have appeared . . . in a country that considers itself to be democratic.'"[9]

In June 2007 Freedom House reported that

New laws on combating terrorism and extremism further opened the door for abuses of civil liberties. A new counterterrorism law includes vague formulations that allow for the banning of any organization that justifies or supports terrorism. Amendments to the law on extremism expand the definition of extremist activities to include slandering a government official in the performance of his duties. Likewise, a new law bars parties from contesting elections if one member is convicted of extremism. Critics of these measures argue that existing laws are already strong enough to address these problems, while the new laws are so vaguely worded that they can be used to silence opposition politicians and the press. Against this background, foreign media reported a number of cases in which opposition-minded activists who crossed the authorities were taken to insane asylums, a common practice during the Soviet era.[10]

Human Rights Watch claims that

It is an appalling fact that 15 years after the collapse of communist totalitarian-
ism in the Soviet Union, numerous individuals are incarcerated in Russia after
politically motivated trials. Dozens of Russian citizens have been thus convicted
and imprisoned, eroding faith in Russia as a nation that respects the freedom of
conscience and the rule of law. No one can accept that Mikhail Khodorkovsky
and Platon Lebedev would be in prison today, had they not exercised their basic
political rights and freedoms. Members of the G-7 must express their concerns
that citizens like Igor Sutyagin (pronounced a "political prisoner" by Amnesty
International), Valentin Danilov, and Mikhail Trepashkin have been convicted
and imprisoned after politically motivated trials, and others—Oscar Kaibyshev
and O. Korobeinichev, seem destined for a similar fate.[11]

Former U.S. Congressman, Tom Lantos, and other political leaders, journalists, and human rights organizations have expressed great concern at the
number of persons who have been imprisoned not for any crimes but for
political activities in recent years in the Russian Federation.

United States

According to Freedom Now, the United States alone among the world's major
governments maintains the fiction that it holds no political prisoners.[12] The
official position is that all those jailed here for politically motivated actions are
"criminals." Yet in all other countries, regardless of the politics of the rulers, it
is an accepted truth that dissenters, jailed for opposing the government, are,
in fact, political prisoners.

By labeling political prisoners as criminals, the U.S. government has also
been able to shield from serious view human rights violations against them.
These include prison sentences longer than in most dictatorships, psychological torture, and brutality including sexual assault.

In 2005, Irene Khan, Amnesty International's general secretary, described
Guantanamo Bay as "the gulag of our time." "Since it was set up in 2002,
the detainment complex at Guantanamo Bay has been the public face of
the Bush administration's semi-secret foreign prison network—a collection of camps, cells, and cages that today holds 437 prisoners. But 'Gitmo'
has always been the tiny showpiece, the jewel in a very dark crown, for a
much larger, less visible foreign network of military detention facilities.
CIA 'black' sites, and outsourced foreign prisons. It is a prison camp that
rightly attracts opprobrium, but it also serves to focus attention away from
shadowy ghost jails, borrowed third-nation facilities, much larger prisons
holding thousands in Iraq, and a full-scale network of detention centers and
prisons in Afghanistan."

Freedom Now attests that we may never know how many secret prisons exist (or, for a time, existed) in the shape-shifting American mini-gulag, but according to the *Washington Post*, some locations for these black sites include itinerant CIA detention centers "on ships at sea," a site in Thailand, and another on "Britain's Diego Garcia island in the Indian Ocean." Uzbekistan has been reported as one possible location, Algeria another. Denials were issued about ghost jails being located in Russia and Bulgaria. The British *Guardian* names "a US airbase in the Gulf state of Qatar" as another suspected site.[13]

As of 2005, Freedom Now claims there are about 150 people locked up in U.S. prisons because of their political actions or beliefs.[14] Among the more famous are:

- Leonard Peltier: After the freedom of information act exposed evidence against his conviction. . . . After the Justice Department admitted in Leonard's second appeal that it had no idea who killed the two FBI agents—a crime for which Leonard is now wrongly serving two life sentences—Leonard still remains a political prisoner in a country that champions political prisoners of other countries.
- Mumia Abu-Jamal: Mumia Abu Jamal has been on death row in Pennsylvania for 17 years, awaiting execution—the only political prisoner on death row. Initially scheduled for execution on August 17, 1995, the execution was stayed by a court order 10 days prior to being carried out. He is currently awaiting a decision from the Supreme Court of Pennsylvania on whether or not he is to receive a new trial.
- Geronimo ji Jaga Pratt, in 1971, a leader in the Black struggle for human rights, was framed on a murder charge in California in 1971. The key witness against him was in the pay of the police. Government spies infiltrated his defense team. Many pages of evidence, proving Geronimo's innocence, were "lost" by government lawyers. It was later revealed that he was a target of the FBI COINTELPRO program which sought to destroy the Black movement. Today, nearly 20 years later, Geronimo is one of the longest held political prisoners in the world.
- In 1984, Susan Rosenberg was arrested and charged with possession of weapons, explosives, and false ID. A white North American woman, Susan has been deeply committed since childhood to struggles for human rights including the movements for Puerto Rican independence, Black liberation, and women's liberation. Although she and her codefendant Tim Blunk were convicted of possessing the materials, not using them, they received sentences of 58 years, the longest ever given on this charge. Susan also endured two years of psychological torture in the Lexington Control Unit before it was closed.

Whether these inmates deserve the title of political prisoners is still under debate. Spokespersons for the Federal Bureau of Prisons maintain that the United States does not have political prisoners. It claims that the persons named above who were actively involved in movements for Native American sovereignty, black liberation, Puerto Rican independence, and against racism, imperialism, women's oppression, and nuclear weapons are common criminals.

Notes

1. Falun Dafa Clearwisdom.net, "Criminal Prisoners Incited to Brutally Torture Ms. Liu Dan in Heilongjiang Province Women's Forced Labor Camp," http://www .clearwisdom.net/emh/articles/2007/4/10/84410.html (accessed June 9, 2008).

2. Government of Tibet in Exile, "Political Prisoners and Prisoners of Conscience," http://www.tibet.com/Humanrights/HumanRights96/hr96-3.html (accessed July 22, 2009).

3. Chinese "Justice" & Detention Centres in Tibet, "Political Prisoner Rights and Chinese "Justice"/Detention Centres in Tibet," http://www.guchusum.org/aboutUS/ ChinesePrisoninTibet/+abid/81/Default.aspx (accessed July 22, 2009).

4. All of the quotations in this section are from the Office of the High Commissioner for Human Rights, "Principles of Medical Ethics relevant to the Role of Health Personnel, Particularly Physicians, in the Protection of Prisoners and Detainees against Torture and Other Cruel, Inhuman or Degrading Treatment or Punishment," http://www.unhchr.ch/html/menu3/b/h_comp40.htm (accessed July 22, 2009).

5. Women's Forum against Fundamentalism in Iran, "Iran's New Strategy to Kill Political Prisoners: Murder in Prison" (September 8, 2006), http://www.wfafi.org/ wfafistatement33.htm (accessed June 24, 2008).

6. https://blythe-systems.com/piopermail/nytr/Week-of-Mon-20040816/0 (accessed June 9, 2008).

7. Addameer Prisoners Support and Human Rights Association, "Torture of Palestinian Political prisoners in Israeli Prisons" (October 2003).

8. Amnesty International, http://asiapacific.amnesty.org/library/index/ENGEUR 4602911996 (accessed August 18, 2008).

9. Grigory Pasko, "Human Rights Congress in Moscow Adopts Resolution," http:// www.robertamsterdam.com/2006/12/girgory_pasko_list_ (accessed August 18, 2008).

10. Freedom House, "Freedom in the World 2007," ID 20515 http://www.ecoi .net/190001::Russian Federation/328797.324720.

11. International Helsinki Federation for Human Rights, ID 15408, http://www .ecoi.net/190001::Russian Federation/328797.324720.

12. "Political Prisoners in the U.S.A.," http://www.totse.com/en/law/justice_for -all/pol-pris.html (accessed September 4, 2008).

13. Nick Turse, "American Prison Planet, the Bush Administration as Global Jailor" (2006).

14. http://www.totse.com/en/law/justice_for_all/pol-pris.html (accessed September 4, 2008).

Appendix B
Tables

TABLE B.1.
Total Prison Population, Rate per 100,000, and Number of Institutions by Country

Country	Prison Population	Rate per 100,000	Number of Institutions
Canada	36,389 (2003)	116	168
United States	2,135,901 (2004)	724	146 (federal), 1,558 (state)
Argentina	44,969 (2004)	148	30 (federal), 136 (provincial)
Brazil	330,642 (2004)	183	868
England	77,421 (2004)	145	140
France	52,908 (2005)	88	185
Germany	80,413 (2004)	97	237
Italy	56,530 (2004)	97	222 (162 remand prisons, 35 prisons, 8 for execution of security measures, 17 juvenile)
Sweden	7,332 (2005)	81	84
Hungary	16,419 (2005)	163	35
Poland	82,954 (2005)	217	213
Russia	819,000 (2005)	547	762 (colonies), 7 (prisons), 62 (juvenile colonies)
Egypt	61,845 (2005)	87	43
Iran	135,132 (2001)	191	184 (156 adult, 28 juvenile)
Israel	13,603 (2004)	209	24
Nigeria	39,153 (2004)	31	147
South Africa	156,175 (2005)	344	225
China	1,548,498 (2004)	118	679 (includes 30 juvenile institutions)
India	322,357 (2002)	31	1,162 (105 central prisons, 296 district prisons, 677 subprisons, 25 open prisons, 13 women's prisons, 12 Borstal schools, 9 juvenile camps, 25 special prisons).
Japan	76,413 (2005)	60	189
Australia	24,171 (2004)	120	124

Source: International Centre for Prison Studies, King's College, London.

TABLE B.2.
Capacity Level and Occupancy Level by Country

Country	Capacity	Occupancy Level (%)
Canada	34,030	95.5
United States	1,951,650	107.6 (112 state prisons; 152 federal prisons)
Argentina	NA	NA
Brazil	180,953	182.7
England	69,498	111.4
France	48,090	110.0
Germany	79,378	99.9
Italy	42,641	134.2
Sweden	7,099	103.3
Hungary	11,400	145.1
Poland	70,002	118.5
Russia	960,066	79.5
Egypt	NA	NA
Iran	65,000	243.1
Israel	13,988	97.2
Nigeria	42,681	92.0
South Africa	113,825	164.1
China	NA	NA
India	229,874	140.2
Japan	72,182	115.9
Australia	20,503	105.9

Source: International Centre for Prison Studies, King's College, London.

TABLE B.3.
Number of Female Prisoners and Percent of Total Inmates

Country	Number of Female Prisoners	% of Total Inmates
Canada	1,819	5.0
United States	185,823	8.7
Argentina	2,608	5.8
Brazil	10,911	3.3
England	4,568	5.9
France	1,958	3.7
Germany	4,101	4.7
Italy	2,657	4.7
Sweden	455	6.2
Hungary	952	5.8
Poland	2,406	2.9
Russia	51,597	6.3
Egypt	2,659	4.3
Iran	71,231	4.6
Israel	313	2.3
Nigeria	744	1.9
South Africa	3,436	2.2
China	71,231	4.6
India	10,315	3.2
Japan	4,508	5.9
Australia	1,668	6.9

Source: International Centre for Prison Studies, King's College, London.

Index

Abu-Jamal, Mumia, 141
abuse, 79–80, 131. *See also* torture
Acacia Prison, Western Australia
    (Australia), 120
"A" class prisoners, 102
administrative detention, 133–34
adult basic education, 18
Africa, 87–97. *See also specific countries*
Afshari, Ali, 135
AGCC. *See* Arthur Gorrie Correctional
    Center, Queensland (Australia)
age of criminal responsibility, 12
Ahalina Center for Egyptian Family
    Support and Development, 134
al-Fayoum Prison (Egypt), 131, 133
Algeria, 141
al-Wdi al-Gadid prison (Egypt), 133
Argentina, 25–28; number of female
    prisoners and percent of total
    inmates, *146*; number of prisons,
    144; parole, 28; population, 25;
    prison capacity and occupancy levels,
    145; prison conditions, 26; prison
    population, 25, *144*; prison staff, 27;
    visitation, 28; women's issues, 26–27,
    146

Arthur Gorrie Correctional Center
    (AGCC), Queensland (Australia),
    119
Asia, 99–111. *See also specific countries*
Association for Human Rights Legal Aid
    (AHRLA), 134
Auburn prison system, 2
Australia, 115–22; ethnic groups, 115;
    incarceration of Indigenous people,
    118; number of female prisoners and
    percent of total inmates, *146*; number
    of prisons, *144*; offenses for which
    prisoners are interred, *116*; parole,
    117–18; population, 115; prison
    capacity and occupancy levels, *145*;
    prison conditions, 116–17; prison
    population, 116, *144*; prison staff,
    116, 117; private prisons, 5, 118–21,
    123; Supermax prison (New South
    Wales), 116; visitation, 118; women's
    issues, 117, *146*

babies, 56. *See also* children; *specific*
    countries
"B" class prisoners, 102
Beccaria, Cesare, 2–3

About the Authors

Rita J. Simon is a University Professor in the Department of Justice, Law, and Society at American University. She is the author of 46 books and the editor of 19 books.

Christiaan A. de Waal works as an investigator and has been involved in several high-profile cases including an international drug case and an antidumping case. Prior to that he worked in public safety for several years. He earned a master of arts degree in international justice and terrorism and a bachelor of arts degree in justice from American University in Washington, DC.

As the son of a Dutch diplomat, Christiaan has lived in numerous countries and is fluent in several languages. He now divides his time between Washington, DC, Europe, and Canada.